L. B Hilles

Chickens Come Home to Roost

A Novel. Thirteenth Edition

L. B Hilles

Chickens Come Home to Roost
A Novel. Thirteenth Edition

ISBN/EAN: 9783337026783

Printed in Europe, USA, Canada, Australia, Japan

Cover: Foto ©Thomas Meinert / pixelio.de

More available books at **www.hansebooks.com**

PHŒBE STRONG.

" *Yes—a spirit pure as hers is always pure, e'en when it errs, as sunshine, broken by the rill, tho' turned aside, is sunshine still.*"

CHICKENS

COME HOME TO ROOST

A NOVEL

THIRTEENTH EDITION.

By
L. B. HILLES

———

Isaac H. Blanchard Co.
PUBLISHERS
NEW YORK

TO

GEORGE P. SMITH,

WHO LOVES A HORSE; WHOSE HEART PULSATES IN A ROYAL
SETTING; WHOSE FIDELITY NEVER FALTERS, AND
WHOSE FRIENDSHIP NEVER FAILS,

THIS VOLUME IS

DEDICATED BY THE AUTHOR.

It is an old lesson, time approves it true,
And those who know it best, deplore it most,
When all is won that all desire to woo,
The paltry prize is hardly worth the cost.

LORD BYRON.

PREFACE.

It is no longer fashionable to encumber books with a preface. Never having observed the rules of fashion, I am, of course, lacking in a proper sense of their value.

As it will sometimes happen that some of the details of a great and imposing architectural pile will escape the observation of many, and therefore fail to excite praise, so perhaps, it may happen that much of this work will meet with a similar fate.

Already, however, I fancy the great business of the reader will be to go about and declare his or her disbelief in the existence of many of the characters I have attempted to portray. Therefore, it seems proper to insist in the very beginning, that the incidents related in this book actually took place, and that there was such a character as Phineas Strong. In that portion of Virginia where he lived, the memory of his good deeds is enshrined in the hearts of his grateful neighbors. His eternal local fame is as assured as is the world fame of Washington and Lincoln. He had a daughter whose name was Phœbe. The incredulous pilgrim may, if inclination prompts, journey to that same little burying ground on the banks of the Rappahannock River, and there find the grave of this same Phœbe, and in the shade of that fragrant cedar, on the silent shaft that throws its soft and tender shadows around the sacred scene, may be still read the inscription loyal affection inspired.

As to the hero of the piece, he, after its publication, may, by means of private pamphlet or public press, demur, traverse, rejoin or plead to many of the allegations on its pages; but, knowing him as I do, as a lover of the truth, I would not be surprised if, as heretofore, he pursued the even tenor of his way, unheard, unnoticed and unsung. Though I have laid before the public eye his character and the secrets of his generous heart, his real name will never be expressed by pen of mine.

Respectfully,
L. B. HILLES.

SOUND BEACH, CONN.

LIST OF ILLUSTRATIONS.

CHICKENS COME HOME TO ROOST.

CHAPTER I.

In that part of Culpepper County, Virginia, where the west bank of the Rappahannock River forms its boundary, and about fifteen miles northwest of Fredericksburg, on the 30th day of April, 1863, there stood, and perhaps still stands, an old-fashioned farmhouse of the Colonial type. It faced the rising sun, and overlooked at the base of a terraced hill the beautiful river as it rippled to the sea. The front of this house was sheltered by a wide porch which extended north and south its extreme length. Ten or twelve massive square pillars supported the roof, which was above the second story. The porch flooring was of oak boards, scrubbed white and smooth. Green blinds, half-closed, shaded a row of windows along the walls, and in the center, a wide old-fashioned door, with narrow windows on either side, a brass knocker in its middle, indicated the means of entrance and exit.

At the north end of this porch, and continuing around the corner to the south until it reached the second pillar, was a lattice work, extending upward ten or twelve feet. Upon this lattice a honeysuckle bush flourished in luxuriant and perfumed extravagance. Its petals had already burst into full bloom, and the zephyr that stirred its leaves with a touch as gentle as a breath was laden with the sweet odors of the vine and the flower.

The silence around was unbroken; a bee, darting in and out of a blossom with a rapidity that defied the quickness of the eye, whirred its wings occasionally, and the sound was like the roaring of a river, so quiet was everything.

It was near to ten o'clock, and the morning sun was far above the bold hills that formed, at this part, the opposite shore of the river. Its warm rays were falling in splendor over the scene. The white walls of the house looked glistening and whiter in the clear sunlight. The large, tall, red chimneys that flanked and seemed to protect the house at either end, shone redder and brighter than ever. The green blinds matched the lilac leaves in the yard, and harmonized with the waving grass that adorned the terraces.

About this scene was an air of neatness rare to see. The wide porch suggested home, and the huge walnut tree, whose mighty limbs shaded its south end and a portion of the house, seemed to invite even the stranger to repose in the seats beneath its foliage. As I said, all was silent. There was no sign of life, human or otherwise, except the aforesaid bee, who was even now entirely buried in a blossom of honeysuckle.

Quietly, suddenly, the door opened, and immediately there came forth a young person of the female sex. I said she was young before I saw her face, because the lightness of her step indicated that only the grace of youth could walk with such fawn-like softness. When she had closed the door, her face came into full view, and reader, on that day I saw the face of one that was destined never to depart from memory. This face belonged to the heroine of my story, and such faces are only seen nowadays in pictures or fanciful lithographs. I am vain enough to attempt a description of this person as I saw her on that day.

She was perhaps eighteen, perhaps twenty, with a form more inclining to tall than short, and yet she was neither tall nor short. Her costume, I confess, looked a little quaint, and my lady readers will no doubt smile when I describe it. Her head was adorned with what we call a poke bonnet, such as we now see worn by members of the Salvation Army. It was made of drab silk, over pasteboard, and had not a flower on it. Broad bands of silk ribbons, tied in a bow beneath her chin, held it in place, and I can assure my lady friends it was adjusted exactly straight. From underneath her bonnet hung two heavy braids of hair, so long as to reach below her middle, and so luxuriant in growth as to appear a little lacking in symmetrical proportions. The color was black, real black, and the texture as soft and as fine as silk. Her dress was a close-fitting bodice, and from it hung two flowing sleeves, then known as bell sleeves; also a skirt of the style of the period, that is, exactly round, and not longer behind than in front, and kept in position and made to swell out by means of a set of rattan hoops. I say rattan, because I often saw these same hoops afterward. This dress was silk and of the color of her bonnet. The position of the dress enabled me to see not only the lady's feet, which were small and finely-formed, but also her ankle, whose delicacy of outline did not fail to suggest the truest and most exact proportions elsewhere. But it was the face I intended to describe.

To begin, her brow was broad and smooth, and not so high as to be intellectual. Her eyebrows, of a luxuriant fringe, were arched and curved beyond the power of art to imitate. Her eyes were large, a deep brown, such eyes as one sees in a gazelle. They were full, lustrous, wide and wondering. Of course, some might have had her nose a little larger. It was, however, exactly straight and exactly regular, and more Grecian than Roman. Her mouth might, I admit, have been smaller to comply with true art, but it was such a pretty mouth that when she smiled, and the corners curved upward and the milk white teeth in two regular rows dazzled before you, you were apt to think this mouth the most inviting you had ever seen. The lips were red and always moist, and if ever a suggestion of kisses was expressed by features, these lips and this mouth expressed it.

But the face—yes, the face; well, it was an oval face, tapering to a chin, that was neither small nor large, but in right proportion, and its point broken by a dimple that spread and grew deeper when she laughed. In color, this face had the most bewitching quality, the most pleasing charm. The brow was whiter than the whitest snow, the cheeks like pure vermilion, and the lower part blending to a delicate pink. I am sure, ladies, though I did not touch it, the skin was as soft as velvet. Her neck was a pillar of whiteness and supported her queenly head with a regal grace. Her form was plump, and her bust development a little more pronounced than an artist would have drawn, yet you would have resented a suggestion to have it lessened.

The bell sleeves, before mentioned, instead of concealing, exposed her lovely arms to the elbows, and through the knitted silk mittens that half-concealed her hands, and reached nearly the length of the arms, you could see the white and red of a lovely skin. From one hand she swung a parasol, or sunshade; and I am afraid my fair critics would have me say this hand was small and dainty. I am telling the truth, and am describing a creature who really lived and moved, and I want to be exact. Her hand, then, was not small. Indeed it was rather a large hand for a woman, and it was plump and red with short fingers, and looked a little as though it was more familiar with household work than with music and painting. It was the face, however, from which the soul of this character was reflected. The large, wondering eyes, the perfect and delicate features, the placid brow, all bespoke innocence, goodness, gentleness.

Her hand and chin may have indicated firmness, but the rest was all womanly, all girlishness, all freshness, all sprightliness. Such was on that day my heroine. She was Phœbe Strong, and was just going out to visit an old colored woman who lived a mile down the river.

CHAPTER II.

BEFORE proceeding to acquaint my readers with the particular purpose Phœbe had in visiting a white-washed cabin on the riverside, I deem it proper to make further observations about the scene to which they have been introduced.

The old-fashioned house was, then, the home and residence of one Phineas Strong. It was nearly in the middle of an estate that lay along the river for a mile north and south, and extended back toward the hills and woods for another mile, comprising in all nearly fifteen hundred acres. Much of it was rich meadow along the river, some hillsides, and a portion a wooded tableland toward the west. Of this estate perhaps six hundred acres consisted of primitive forest. From its position on an elevation somewhat back, the house commanded a magnificent view up and down the river and beyond into Fauquier and Stafford Counties.

The place had long been known as River View, and was in many respects an elegant, old-fashioned, Virginia country home. In addition to the mansion, which, large and roomy and full two stories and attic high, there was a large stone barn to the left and south, a large carriage house, also of stone, a large smoke house, of red brick, a blacksmith shop, several corn cribs, a spacious sty for pigs, some distance from the barn, and toward the river.

Directly in front of the house, nestling half-hidden under a little hill, and at the foot of a huge button-wood or sycamore tree, was a long, low building, called the dairy. It was also of stone. A well-beaten path led direct to this spot, and at its terminus was a spring of sparkling water, which bubbled perpetually at the door of the spring house and flowed over a sanded and pebbled floor in the interior; thence discharged itself from the other side, whence it went falling and leaping from terrace to terrace, and from rock to rock till it mingled with the waters of the Rappahannock, a quarter of a mile away.

All of these buildings were white, in a recent coating of lime. The fences which inclosed them were also white. The gates were all on their hinges. There were no loose palings, no broken boards. There was no litter in the yard and no débris on the grass plots. The shade, fruit, and ornamental trees were neatly trimmed into various artistic shapes, and the whole surroundings indicated thrift, neatness, plenty, taste, elegance, and peace. There was not another house, except the cabin to which Phœbe was directing her steps, within a mile's distance. A driveway in front of the house led to a gateway about three hundred yards to the south, which opened upon a country road that crossed the river at a point where there was a passable and safe fording. This road led directly through the estate, and while it belonged absolutely to and was kept in order by its owner, custom from time immemorial had sanctioned its use by the public.

From the description of River View the reader may, perhaps, form some idea of the character of its occupants.

The present owner was a Quaker, and had now lived here nearly twenty years. Why he located there and why he was content to remain, were then, and perhaps are now, subjects of never ending speculation.

Many remembered when Phineas Strong first moved into the neighborhood. He came to Fredericksburg by boat from somewhere north. Some said from Philadelphia, but others are positive he came from Reading; still others that he came from New York.

His family consisted of himself, his wife, four boys and a baby in arms, a girl, who in time became our heroine, Phœbe.

Phineas Strong dressed then and until he died in the garb of his religion. He used the plain language on all occasions, and to every one.

In person he was tall, broad shouldered, had a fine, well rounded head, covered with a wealth of dark brown hair, curling, and falling in waves to his coat collar. His face and form reminded many of the pictures of George Washington. His eyes were blue, and had a tender expression which spoke volumes for the goodness of his heart. His countenance, however, was placid, serene and ruddy. He looked then, and twenty years after, the picture of health, unruffled content, and a splendid physical manhood.

His wife was rather diminutive in size and stature. Her costume complied with the rules of her religion, but her face, which shone out from her Shaker bonnet, was as sweet and as placid as a day in May. Hardly a shadow could be detected, and though you might gaze into her brown eyes forever the expression was always one of affection and peace. She looked the sweet wife and ideal mother; and it was remarked by many how closely she strained little Phœbe to her bosom on the morning she walked down the gangplank from the steamer to the shore. She had never seen River View until that morning twenty years ago. Phineas had purchased it because he liked it. She never even inquired where it was. If it suited Phineas it would suit her. She had no life, no plans apart from her husband, and where he was, there she was content.

He helped her and the baby from the carriage when they arrived in front of that grand, wide old porch, waved his hand toward the flowing river, and said: "How does thee like the place, Rachel?"

"I think it is lovely, Phineas. I am sure we will all be very happy here."

An old colored woman who had been born on the place welcomed her, and led her and the four boys into the house.

This was the beginning of the life of most of my characters at River View, who have contrived to make it a famous spot, and who have achieved more or less distinction in the pages that are to follow.

CHAPTER III.

RIVER VIEW had once been the estate of Benjamin Porter, whose name is carved in rude letters upon a large stone that is set in the east wall just over the wide door with the brass knocker. This stone bears date 1767. It may still be seen, and suggests to the beholder many things besides the vanity of the builder.

North of this mansion is a plot of ground surrounded by a white board fence and adorned with boxwood and cedar trees. It is the family burying ground. All the tombstones then contained the name of Porter, but, up to the opening of my story, not a grave had been dug in it since 1822. In the month of March, that year, the 17th, I think the tombstone says, the remains of David Porter, aged thirty-three, were laid to rest. Inquiry will enlighten him who is curious of the fact that David Porter was the grandson of the founder of River View, and that on or about the said 17th day of March, 1822, he was shot in a quarrel with his brother, William Porter, in a dispute as to which should receive the favors of Miss Letitia Edwards, a Fauquier County belle, who lived some miles up the river.

It seem Miss Edwards loved the one who was killed, and, upon learning the truth of the situation, the murderer fled the country.

These two inherited the property jointly. Their mother and only sister being dead, and there being no contestants, the surviving brother necessarily took the entire estate. For many years he managed, by means of correspondence, the affairs of the property, and through the fidelity of one of his father's slaves kept it in good repair and prosperous. But one day the old slave died, and the place began to run down. The taxes were unpaid, and things went from bad to worse. At last word came that William Porter, the owner, had died in a Northern city. The whole property was about to escheat to the State, no heirs having appeared, when Phineas Strong arrived at the Court House, and filed for record a warranty deed purporting to have been executed by William Porter, bachelor, in consideration of five thousand dollars—a paltry sum even at that time.

Strong paid the taxes, and proceeded to take possession. There were hints at times that his title was bad and that other heirs would come some day and claim the property, but to these he paid no attention. Porter had owned the property uninterruptedly from 1822 to 1843, and the Strongs had now been in quiet possession for twenty years. It would seem that Phineas Strong might rest secure on that point. The estate had, however, under his management become valuable, and yearly products of wheat and tobacco had given him more than a competence. Indeed, Strong, unlike most of his neighbors, was rich in both lands and money. He had, however, no slaves, nor had he ever any. He was not in sympathy with the people and customs about

him.   He was neither religious nor social.   He had no
political aspirations, and now was heartily in sympathy with the Union.

His peculiarities were marked in other ways.   He
was known to be rich, and was often appealed to by his
neighbors for loans.   As securities for the sums, which
he never refused, he was offered mortgages upon slaves.
These he never accepted.   Then, he never charged his
patrons any interest, and this, instead of resounding to
his credit, was often the subject of adverse criticism.
Some impugned his motives, and others said he had
once committed some great sin, and did such things to
appease a guilty conscience.   However, all in need
were quick to appeal to his ready purse, and all were
equally positive that the man was either a crank or a
rogue.   But as none of these observations reached the
ears of Phineas Strong, he lived among them twenty
years, mentally at ease, happy, prosperous, above envy,
above want, fearless, generous, and exact.

CHAPTER IV.

In order that the reader may a little better understand the conduct of some of my characters, I will remind him or her that the Civil War was now in progress, and for more than two years all of that part of
Virginia in the vicinity of the home of my heroine was
one vast battlefield, the scenes already of conflicts past
and conflicts to come between the grand armies of the
North and the brave and persistent ones of the South.

Phineas Strong was an abolitionist, and his sympathy was with the Union, but as all of his neighbors
were already enlisted in the Southern cause, his position and sentiments provoked no open hostility. His
religious training, in a measure, restrained his real impulses, as there is no doubt but for these the retreat at
Bull Run, which chagrined him terribly, would have
found him a volunteer in the Union Army. His personal courage was unquestioned, and as his sentiments
were never concealed, few expected that he would remain passive during the conflict. His age, now sixty-
two, may have, of course, restrained his natural ardor,
and his love of home, of wife, his affection for Phœbe,
have influenced him in his course. But those who
know the hereditary influences that exist among the

Quaker sect against the shedding of human blood, will
perhaps understand why he forbore to take up arms.

There was one other reason that might have excused
him. The four boys mentioned in the second chapter,
Robert, George, Ephraim and Edward, had all gone
just as soon as they heard the firing of the guns at Bull
Run. He witnessed their riding away, each on his
horse, and never said them nay. At that battle Robert
had fallen, and he and Phœbe had gone to the front
the morning after the fight and found his body, face
down, his head toward the enemy. They brought it
home, and it was laid in the little family burying
ground, already described.

It was a source of quiet consolation, despite his great
grief, that Phineas Strong found his son's remains on
the battlefield with his face to the foe. He said to
Rachel when he laid the corpse on the bier in the front
room, "Mother, Robbie wasn't running away when he
fell."

Ephraim, George and Edward were now encamped
with Burnside's army, some miles down the river; but,
as between their home and camp, a long line of Confederate pickets, reaching from the Rapidan to near
Fredericksburg, extended, communications by visits
between these young loyal soldiers and their home were
completely cut off. Mails there were, but these were
uncertain, and absolutely beyond the reach of the boys
in blue. Various expedients and schemes were therefore employed by the brothers to send messages of love
and encouragement to Phœbe and their mother.

At this time there extended and was in occasional operation a backwater canal along the Rappahannock River from Fredericksburg to Kelly's Mills. This canal, ruins of which still exist, was used before the war to transport flour and other freight down the river to tide water at Fredericksburg. The Strong boys had often sailed down this canal on the flat-bottomed boats manned by slaves. At intervals along the route were locks for lowering or raising the boats. At these locks was generally a keeper or toll collector. The keeper was usually a slave, and occupied a hut or cabin on the bank of the river near the scene of his duties.

Just above where the road referred to entered the river there stood, and perhaps still stands, the white-washed cabin of the lock keeper. The locks were there at the time my story opens, and occasionally canal boats, by the aid of slaves and poles, made their way up and down the river. Among the slaves who had the confidence of his master to an unlimited extent was a swarthy black giant named George, the property of Mr. Kelly, up the river. George was so honest that his master would trust him to take a boat load of flour to Fredericksburg, and receive the money for it. George was never known to lie or steal.

In the cabin near the locks on Strong's place lived, and had lived from a time whereof the memory of man runneth not back to the contrary, a colored woman named Dinah. Dinah was of huge frame, and of powerful muscular development. No one knew how old she was. She had swung the locks herself, and could do it with ease in slack water and in flood. In his trips black George and big Dinah necessarily became acquainted, and between the two there sprang up a warm and lasting affection. Many and many a time in the early dawn George would pole his boat into the locks, and as it glided noiselessly along, drink a cup of steaming coffee and swallow an immense slice of corn bread which Dinah would pass to him. Then as the boat swung into the stream, you could hear him say, "Recon that's po'erful good coffee, Miss Dinah. They ain't none up the river like that, suah!"

Dinah was there when the Strongs came. She said she was there "Long 'fore dem Porters; rec'n she belonged to Mar's Porter."

Phineas Strong told her she was free, and handed her a piece of paper with writing to that effect.

She took the document, held it upside down, then crosswise, pretending to read it through, then said: "Dis heah paper doan tell me whar Ise to go. Guess I'll show it to Geauge when he comes down de river, and find out if it's right."

She showed it to George, and ten minutes after her interview she was standing at the back door of the Strong mansion waiting to see the man who made her free.

"What is it, Dinah?" he asked.

"Dis heah paper, Geauge says, makes me a free woman, and if I take it I'll have to leave the country or have to pay yer to let me stay, or you'll have to pay me, or like dat. Enny way, if Mas'r Strong will jes take dis heah back, and jes let ole Dinah stay in de cabin, den Dinah be berry much 'bleeged, an' Mas'r Strong won't never want for fish, if dey is enny in de riber. Ole Dinah got rheumatiz, can't walk away, 'deed I can't; besides, I neber said I wanted freedom, nohow, 'taint no good, Geauge done say so, and says I mus' give dis back, so here it is."

With that she pushed the paper into Strong's hands. He assured her she was welcome to remain, but advised her to keep the paper. This she positively refused, saying "Geauge" told her not to "tech" it. It was not until he had promised to keep it till she called for it, that the old negress showed willingness to depart.

This was about the experience he had with all the slaves that remained on the place. In spite of his efforts to free them, they not only refused to be free, but begged to be allowed to remain. So, in spite of his principles, he was still the master of ten or twelve helpless, dependent black people.

Between old Dinah and the Strong children the warmest and tenderest feeling prevailed. She regarded Phœbe as little less than an angel, and for the boys, there was never a time, if called upon, that she would not have laid down her life.

It was, therefore, no sooner learned by Dinah that the Strong boys were at Fredericksburg than she acquainted "Geauge" with the fact. If George had any ties approaching tenderness other than those for Dinah and her coffee, they were for her friends, the Strongs.

When, therefore, Dinah entrusted him with a bundle

of good things on his next trip down the river, with strict instructions to find "dem boys," and give them "Missy's letters" and not "cum back till he did," George regarded this as a sacred trust, and there is no doubt he would have performed his mission had the difficulty and danger been ten times as great. He was now due at the Strong ford on his return, indeed, he was expected by Dinah by "sun up," but she had been early at the mansion with a string of fresh fish, and had apprised the expectant Phœbe that "Geauge" had not "dun showed up." About ten o'clock, therefore, not hearing from Dinah, Phœbe's anxiety and impatience could no longer be controlled. She donned the costume, heretofore described, and started for the cabin to see if black George had returned with letters of love from her brothers, who were exposed to the dangers of war.

CHAPTER V.

Though the war had already lasted two years, and the country around was full of armies, and within a few miles of where she now stood had been fought a great battle, Phœbe had really seen but few soldiers, and none had ever molested the house or its inmates. The Strongs had been appealed to but little either by the Confederates or the Union soldiers, and though, in the very midst of war and battle and the clash of arms, were as yet comparative strangers to their awful ravages.

Phœbe had proceeded about fifty yards along the graveled driveway, intent only on reaching Dinah's cabin, oblivious to her surroundings, and so preoccupied with her thoughts that she failed to notice the big gate ahead had swung open, and a company of Union soldiers, carrying a flag, were marching toward her. They had now approached within thirty feet, when the tattoo of a drum aroused her to a sense of the situation. She was face to face with the color bearer of the company, the captain and the beater of the tattoo, who, strange to relate, was a boy not over twelve years of age.

Phœbe gave expression to an "Oh, my!" stepped

back and to one side. The captain shouted, "Halt! Salute!"

Immediately the company came to a standstill. Every cap was doffed, every form inclined to the beauteous Phœbe, and every hand waved a respectful salute. Phœbe was now crimson with blushes, which must have added vastly to her natural beauty. The captain, cap in hand, bowing for the second time, advanced a step, and with a voice about as sweet as any Phœbe had ever heard, said:

"I beg your pardon, miss, if we frightened you. We are soldiers, marching since morning, thirsty, hungry, weary. Your surroundings tempted us. Your shade trees looked so inviting, your big house so homelike, we could not resist the temptation to invade your retreat, and ask permission to at least quench our thirst and rest from the noonday heat. We will do you no harm, and will cheerfully pay for any food you may be pleased to part with."

Phœbe was at first disposed to be frightened, but the captain's manner and voice so reassured her that she summed up courage to say:

"My brothers are all soldiers in the Union army, and if you gentlemen are really Union soldiers (they were so covered with dust that they looked like Confederates), I am sure my father will be delighted to extend you all the hospitality in his power."

Phœbe felt sure they were Union men, but the color bearer had now folded his flag, and the captain's regimentals looked travel stained. He assured her they were soldiers, good and true, and added:

"My name is Captain Charles Barr, Company K, Second Delaware Volunteers. There are sixty-six of us. Our division, under General Howard, passed here this morning" (which it had, unknown to any one at that time). "We were left in the rear to guard stores, and blaze part of the line of march. We have been delayed by Confederate cavalry, but hope to reach our division before night."

Phœbe led the way, and very soon the entire company were disposed under the trees on that part of the lawn between the dairy and the house. Phineas Strong appeared, and very soon after the entire colored force about the place was carrying bread and ham and milk to the hungry.

The little drummer boy, unobserved by the others, had made his way to the porch, and was now stretched full length upon the boards, sound asleep.

While the soldiers ate and drank, Phœbe learned from Captain Barr that her three brothers were in General Howard's division, known as the Eleventh Corps, and had passed within two miles of the house that very morning; that the Union forces under General Joseph E. Hooker were concentrating near Chancellorsville; that already a large army was in the rear of General Lee, who was intrenched near Fredericksburg, and that a great battle would be fought before many days between these two armies.

The soldiers were now ready to depart, and to the cry of "Fall in! fall in!" all sprang from the ground and formed in line four abreast. Captain Barr was about to give the "Forward, march," when some one called out, "Where's our drummer boy?"

"Where's Robbie?" asked another.

"Hold, captain," said the sergeant, "our drummer boy is not here."

A search ensued among the trees and under the bushes, but the litte felllow was not to be found. The color bearer above referred to was of all the most anxious, and began a loud call for "Robbie," whose drum he had found near the base of the sycamore. At this juncture Phœbe appeared upon the scene, leading Robbie by the hand. She had discovered him asleep and refrained from waking him until the inquiry had become general. She was now brushing his brown curls from his face, and having arrived at the van of the small procession, begged the captain to censure her for the delay and forgive the little fellow. The color bearer, however, seemed disposed to scold, and bluntly told Robbie to fall in.

The boy pulled off his cap as he attempted to adjust his drum, and said:

"Pap, the lady was kind to me; see, she has filled my pockets with sandwiches and given me this bottle of milk."

"This is my pap," said the boy, addressing Phœbe.

Phœbe smiled: the color bearer doffed his cap, and said:

"Sergeant Porter,—Benjamin Porter, of the Second Delaware. This is my boy, Robbie—would run away— followed me to the war, was at my side at Fair Oaks,

Gaines' Mill and Fredericksburg. Won't stay in the rear, miss. Can't do anything with him—broke his mother's heart, I guess. I wish you hadn't found him. He'll be killed some day."

"Attention!" shouted Captain Barr. "Forward, march!"

The gallant captain drew his sword, waved it before him in the sunlight, turned to make a smiling adieu to the Quakers; the fifer played "Yankee Doodle," the boy struck the drum, the color bearer waved his flag, and the little band, dusty but refreshed, marched gayly down the graveled drive.

For some reason which she could not explain, Phœbe strained her eyes after the little drummer boy, till his form was lost in the distance and had disappeared in the shadows of the tall pines.

CHAPTER VI.

THE last sounds of the departing company had completely died away, and the stillness of the morning had again prevailed when Phœbe turned and walked slowly toward the house. There was no need now to go to Dinah's. Black George could come and go, but in the absence of messages from her brothers he had just then no interest for her. Her mind was filled with forebodings, inspired, no doubt, by the information obtained from the soldiers. Another battle! three brothers doomed to be participants; one already a victim; truly her thoughts were not calculated to induce merriment.

Phœbe had much more cause for congratulation than sorrow. Nevertheless, her heart was heavy and her meditations in complete harmony.

The Civil War, to her mind, no matter what its purpose, was wrong. If it had for its object the freeing of the poor slaves, she was confident that they were insensible to either the woes of slavery or the benefits of freedom. If its purpose was to preserve, or rather to reunite, the Union she felt quite sure so far, it had failed in its design. My readers may condemn in Phœbe this apparent lack of enthusiasm for a cause which, just at that time, was occupying the entire thought of a great nation, as well as consuming its treasury.

And here I must beg the reader's pardon for a few moments, and digress in the advancement of my story, to observe that Phœbe was, after all, a very sensible girl. Her conclusions as to the war were certainly warranted by the facts. A number of bloody battles had been fought, and so far the South had been the victor, and had now in the field a larger and better army than ever before. True, Phœbe had lost a brother, but one hundred thousand other brothers were already dead upon the battlefield, and this thought heightened her disdain for the whole scheme of warfare. She wished it over, that her brothers might be home. Had they not been engaged, Phœbe's interest in the great conflict would have been small. As it was, she had kept herself thoroughly posted as to the progress, campaigns, and battles of the great armies in Virginia. She had cried with humiliation over the story of the first battle of Bull Run, and was free to express herself as to the incompetency of General McDowell and quick to praise the intrepid Jackson and the gallant Mc-Laws. When the result of the second battle at the same place was known, she was also loud in her praise of Longstreet and Johnston.

Like others, Phœbe knew all about the puerile efforts of McClellan to take Richmond. She could not repress a smile when the efforts of some of his admirers to praise his retreat as a masterly military movement, unexampled in the history of warfare, ancient or modern, appeared in the Northern papers which found their way to her father's house. And if my reader will again pardon the digression, McClellan's whole campaign, had it not been so sorrowful, was, in the light of all the facts, the most laughable of the war.

The spectacle of a great army of one hundred thousand men, fully accoutered, amply provisioned and appointed, with thousands of cattle and endless trains of stores and ammunition, retreating before an army of sixty thousand, not half as well equipped, must, to a man of lively imagination, have indeed been the subject of congratulation and praise.

Of course the Union forces made a bold stand at Malvern Hill, but this was a position of great natural advantage; and because Lee, who for seven days had been fighting on the offensive, and had driven the Union forces from six battles, with less than fifty thousand men, failed to dislodge an army of eighty thousand, we are told this fight was a grand national victory. As a matter of fact, the Union army had retreated as far as it could, and had to fight the battle of Malvern Hill, or fall into the James River at Harrison's Landing.

It was at Malvern Hill that the Northern soldiers did the fighting, and threatened with death many a cowardly officer if he dared display the "white feather."

McClellan never got done trying to explain why he did not take Richmond; and, why, if he won the battle of Malvern Hill, he did not follow Lee's army, and whip it two or three more times the next day. The gunboats at Harrison's Landing, under whose protecting shelter he rested, no doubt suggested greater military glory.

The glory of the war up to the present time had done much to bring out the incompetency of the Northern generals, and demonstrate the energy, ability, bravery and certainty of the Southern.

Up to this time the Army of the Potomac, having its commander changed after every battle, had met only disaster, defeat, and humiliation. True, Antietam had been fought, and because its one hundred and twenty thousand soldiers repelled the efforts of seventy or eighty thousand, it was called a victory. It was, as a matter of fact, a defeat, as was Malvern Hill, as was afterwards Gettysburg.

In war there is no victory that accomplishes nothing. For McClellan to allow Lee to escape at Antietam, and for Meade to suffer the same thing at Gettysburg, were exhibitions of incompetency, as well as confessions of cowardice.

Burnside at Fredericksburg had found himself at the close of one dull day in December, after a fearful contest with that peerless genius, Robert E. Lee, very much "hors de combat," and, of course, was immediately relieved of his command. These were some of the situations that now presented themselves to the mind of Phœbe. It is not, however, my purpose, reader, to write a criticism upon the War of the Rebellion. This is to be a love story, the heroine already known, and the hero now about to be introduced.

CHAPTER VII.

THE morning of May 1, 1863, will no doubt be long remembered. Men — brave men — women — noble women for the first time in their experiences played grand parts in the drama of life. To loftier pens than mine has fallen the task to laud the few. After that and the three succeeding days history's page was crowded and burnished with the glorious deeds of the fortunate brave. In those four days, between Chancellorsville and Fredericksburg, between the old Inn and Banks' Ford, back in the woods toward the Rapidan, and along and across the old plank road, and up and down the Orange Turnpike, two hundred thousand men and thirty thousand horses fought, were fighting, did fight, the greatest battle of all history. This battle was fought within a few miles of the scene of my story, and before nine o'clock the first day there was more excitement in the Strong home than there had been in the twenty years they had lived there. Here was war, murderous war, right at their threshold. This alone was sufficient cause for concern, but to their dismay and grief, the Strongs had to endure that agony and suspense which came with the knowledge that three sons and brothers were exposed to the dangers of battle. The roar of artillery, and at times the sound of small

HE TOOK THE COLORS FROM HIS STRICKEN FATHER.

arms, was not only sufficient to keep Phœbe and her mother within doors, but to drive all the servants to the woods; not all, for black Dinah remained and waited for the faithful "Geauge."

George never returned.

Reader, I did not witness the battle of Chancellorsville, nor did I see Stonewall Jackson fall from his horse, pierced by the bullets of his own soldiers. I did not see General Hooker fall, stunned by a rifle ball, on the porch of the old Chancellor house. In fact, I saw none of these things. True, I have walked all over the battlefield, and imagined that at this point my father fell; that it was just here Edward Strong was struck by a shell, and that, as he fell, his brother George sprang forward to catch him in his arms, and received in his own breast a charge that laid the two brothers side by side. It was here that Robbie Porter took the colors from his stricken father, and held them aloft until he was borne from the field by main force. Perhaps, at this intrenchment Phœbe's brother Ephraim, a little in advance of his brave comrades, was made a prisoner. These things really happened in this battle, but with the exception of Robbie Porter's startling act, I could never fix the exact spot where the events occurred. Robbie pointed out to me the very place he held the national colors in the air while the Confederates riddled them to shreds with bullets. This battle lasted four days. One hundred and thirty-two thousand soldiers comprised the Union army, and less than sixty thousand the Confederate. Yet, on Tuesday morning, May

5th, the Grand Army of the Potomac, commanded by that grand commander, Joseph Hooker, was diligently seeking some way to escape from Lee's fighting heroes.

The stragglers and deserters were fleeing in droves past the Strong mansion all day Tuesday, and from them Phineas Strong learned that the Union army was whipped, and a general retreat would take place that day, or in the evening. Sure enough, a division of Sedgwick's corps crossed the river just below old Dinah's cabin, and before dawn of the 6th the entire Union forces had vanished from the bloody field of Chancellorsville, leaving more than twenty thousand killed, wounded and prisoners. The rain, which had set in the evening of the 5th, continued most of the 6th; yet Phœbe and her father, mounted on horses, accompanied by Dinah on foot, and two or three faithful blacks, were early on their way to the scene of battle.

To get through the lines, be allowed to look for his sons, and if necessary search for their remains on the field, to penetrate as far as possible within the Confederate lines without attracting attention, Phineas Strong and his little party proceeded to Chancellorsville by a circuitous route through the woods and in a few hour, drenched to the skin, covered with mud, suddenly emerged into the clearing and were laboriously proceeding in the direction of the Chancellor house, when they were just as suddenly surrounded by a dozen Confederate soldiers and commanded to "halt."

The spectacle of a man in Quaker dress, a pretty girl, in a drab riding habit and a silk poke bonnet splashed with red clay, spotted with rain, and three or four shrinking, muddy, barefooted "niggers," trembling in the background, surprised these Confederates far more just then than had they suddenly beheld Sedgwick's entire corps before them.

A drum beat an alarm, and quicker than I can write it, the little party was the concern of the entire regiment.

There is always something, however, in the face of a good and pretty woman which not only arrests attention, disarms danger, but commands homage. Phbœe's face, therefore, was the talisman to safety. Nearly every ragged hat was already doffed, and every gun, before raised, now yielded to the command, "Ground arms."

To Phineas Strong, an officer, evidently a captain, spoke:

"Sir, you will please give the pass word, countersign, or show a pass to proceed within our lines, otherwise we cannot suffer you to continue."

"Friend," said Phineas, "of the rules of war and its cruel and rigid conditions we know but little. We know neither signs nor pass words. We have no pass. We are natives here, and live on the banks of the river, six or seven miles distant. I am Phineas Strong. In this battle, in Howard's or Sedgwick's corps I had three sons—three brave sons, so brave, friend, that I know they are still here. I and my daughter, with our servants, but ask to be allowed to search this battlefield for their remains. We are unarmed, a people of peace. For more than two years I have fed and housed the needy of both armies. From the battlefield of Bull Run I have already borne my oldest son, and he lies buried at our home. To take to their waiting mother the other three is our only purpose."

There was so much frankness, so much pathos in this that nearly all who heard it turned aside to conceal their emotion. They were all soldiers. Soldiers are brave, and brave men have tender hearts.

"What you ask, old man," said the captain, "is impossible. Besides, Sedgwick's corps was cut to pieces, and most of his dead were buried two days ago. The wounded have all been taken away——"

"And the prisoners?" asked Phineas.

"Gone to Richmond," said the captain.

"Who commands thy division or brigade?"

"General Lee, Robert E. Lee."

"And will thee not permit me to see General Lee?"

"My friend, General Lee is the general-in-chief. He would not, he could not, see you! The rules of war are not only rigid but harsh. Suspicion attaches to every one. Caught in our lines, without identification papers, under the rules of war, you are a spy, and it becomes my duty to tell you that you not only cannot search this battleground for dead Union soldiers, but you cannot leave it unless you satisfy us that you are what you claim. Personally, as a man, I believe every word you say. As a soldier, I doubt all; and as a military necessity, I must order you to dismount, and accompany me to headquarters."

"Friend," said Phineas, "thy face indicates a good heart, and thy words are the harshness of military life. Thou mayest request me to dismount, but Phineas Strong takes orders from no man!" With this remark he sat upright in his saddle.

Phœbe, giving a supplicating glance to those around, urged her horse forward to his side, and whispered something in an undertone. At which the old gentleman proceeded to alight, and handing his reins to a servant, he signified his willingness to accompany the captain. Leaving Phœbe to the mercy of her captors, Phineas, the captain, and a small detachment of soldiers proceeded to the tent of General A. P. Hill.

That gentleman, upon hearing the captain first, and the Quaker next, promptly ordered Phineas to the guardhouse, and going himself to gaze upon the young lady, immediately provided her with a bodyguard, and directed that she and her servants be conducted to River View, promising at the same time that her father should be liberated and returned in safety, before sunset, provided his soldiers reported his story true.

With a heavier heart than ever, and with her lustrous eyes swimming in tears, Phœbe was compelled to return home without news of her brothers and with sad news to her waiting, watching mother.

CHAPTER VIII.

THE party had proceeded without incident by the
regular road to within a mile of their destination,
when, without warning or expectation, they came to a
standstill. The cause of the interruption was a small
boy, bareheaded, coatless, with ragged shirt, mud-and-
blood bespattered trousers, shattered shoes and a face as
white as a sheet. He was standing by the roadside,
sobbing, and trying to talk at the same time.

Phœbe, who, during the entire march was so completely absorbed in her own griefs as to be almost oblivious to everything, now raised her head, and looked
toward the sobbing picture of wretchedness in the road-
way. In the pale face and matted hair she recognized
the drummer boy of Company K, Second Delaware,
who had so interested her a few days before. In an instant she was by his side. All the tenderness of an
affectionate heart immediately found expression in her
face, and was reflected in her voice. She was alive
with sympathy, and quickly assured her escort that the
little fellow was her friend. She inquired the cause of
his grief, and between his sobs, learned that his father
was fatally wounded, that he himself had carried the
colors until they were shot from his hands; that after
the retreat was ordered he had gone in search of his

THE DRUMMER-BOY OF CHANCELLORSVILLE.

father, that he had at last found him, deserted and alone, left for dead; that in the darkness of the night, his father, weak and dying, with his assistance, had walked and crawled to this point; that about an hour before he had died, and his body, covered with wet leaves, with his knapsack still under his head, was now lying a few paces distant.

The little fellow begged the soldiers to assist him in the burial of the body, and promised to allow them to make him a prisoner of war as a consideration.

Phœbe bade Dinah and another servant go with the boy and bring to the roadside the corpse of his father.

They found the dead soldier, Robbie's coat spread over his face, and bore it tenderly to the presence of their mistress. Robbie followed, carrying his father's knapsack upon his shoulders, and his belt and pistol on his arm. In the presence of the dead, sympathy and awe are the strongest sensations.

A rough bier was soon prepared, and at Phœbe's direction the whole party, the drummer boy, and the dead soldier, were soon before the white walls and green lawn of River View.

Rachel Strong was wearily waiting their arrival. Her heart sank when she saw the bier—they brought Robbie home that way—and sank lower when she failed to recognize the tall form of her husband. Phœbe almost fell into the good woman's arms, and wet, bedraggled, weeping, sobbed out in gulps and jerks the melancholy incidents that had befallen their trip.

The rain was falling fast, and the dark clouds sailing

to the west promised no immediate indication of sunshine.   The rain, in Virginia, however, on the sixth of
May is warm, and when it falls the young corn swells
and erects its expanding blades and graceful shoots, with
vigor and with pride.

To bury the heroic color bearer was the first concern
of these two estimable and tender women.   A grave
was therefore prepared in the little burying ground,
and to it the soldier was carried.   A rude pine box,
made hastily by one of the colored help, was his coffin.
The mourners were Robbie, Rachel and Phœbe Strong.

This done, the soldiers, who had assisted in every
possible way, and satisfied that the prisoner held by
General Hill was an innocent and harmless Quaker,
took their departure, promising that he should be discharged at once.

The clouds parted in the afternoon, the sun came out,
and at the same time Phineas Strong rode into his own
dooryard.   He commended Phœbe for her conduct
toward the dead soldier and his brave son.   He asked
to see the little fellow, and was shown into the big
parlor, where, curled up on the sofa, covered with a
shawl Phœbe had thrown over him, reposed the boy.
He looked into the face of the sleeping child with an
expression very much like tenderness and admiration.

"Poor child, poor child; another orphan, the heritage
of this dreadful war.   Some mother's heart is breaking
for him.   Phœbe, some wife's heart will break when
she reads the list of the missing!   What did thee say
his name is?"

"Robbie Porter," said Phœbe.

"And his father's?"

"Benjamin Porter," she replied.

"Benjamin Porter," repeated Phineas. "Why, Phœbe, that is the name on the stone above our door!'

"Yes," said Phœbe, "and it seems strange, after ɛ century, another Benjamin should come here to be buried in our little graveyard."

"Well! well," said Phineas, "and was he a young man?"

"Forty, at least," said Phœbe.

"And the boy," he said, turning away, "how old is he?"

"He said he was twelve last October."

"And did he tell thee how in the world he got in the army?"

"He said," continued Phœbe, "that he ran away from home two years ago, in order to be with his father. That he has been in many battles, and has heard from home but seldom. That his mother, he thinks, lives in Philadelphia, and that he has one sister somewhat older. He loved his father dearly and cried himself sick when we buried him."

"To-morrow," said Phineas, "we will start him on his way home."

The sun went down and Robbie slept, and when it arose the next day he was still sleeping. The battle of Chancellorsville had kept him awake too long, and its terrible privations had brought complete exhaustion to this little hero of my story.

CHAPTER IX.

BUT all sleeps come to an end; it is said that even the sleep of death ends in a glorious awakening. Robbie's was the sleep of life, and before its conclusion the natural vigor of a healthy boyhood had returned, and was expressed in his cheeks. The rain-matted hair dried, and his brown locks curled gracefully around his forehead. A soft step in the room awoke him. Phœbe opened one of the window blinds, and as she turned toward the couch, a flood of rare, warm sunshine followed and fondly enveloped her form.

Robbie opened his eyes. At first they blinked a little, but finally got completely opened, and immediately became fastened upon Phœbe's.

I cannot now explain why it was that Phœbe's color heightened just a trifle at this frank, boyish gaze, but it did. That a brown-eyed woman of twenty should blush because a blue-eyed boy of thirteen gave her an ardent and admiring gaze may appear to the reader as bordering too much upon the realm of fiction. It is a fact, nevertheless, and I want the reader to know now that I do not propose to tell anything but the facts in my story. At the time, perhaps, neither Phœbe, certainly not Robbie, thought anything of this incident. In after years both of them thought of it—ah, yes, and un-

derstood it, too. But, now—here was a refined, delicate, beautiful woman, with a heart overflowing with
tenderness, good to this homeless, fatherless boy just
because—because, well, because his situation perhaps
appealed to her. And here was a wild, untamed, daring boy, a lawless product of a great city, already beyond parental restraint, already a wanderer, dirty,
ragged, and, from his talk, completely illiterate, the .
associate of rough, reckless men, indifferent to blood
and death, and as familiar with gun and sword as most
boys are with tops and marbles.

For more than two years this little fellow had not
slept in a bed or eaten at a table. For more than two
years he had worn the few clothes he had on, day and
night continually. For more than two years he had,
in spite of orders, been sneaking in battles by the side
of his father, and had never ceased to hope that some
day he would have an opportunity to kill a "rebel."
For more than two years his had been the companionship of men who drank, swore, chewed tobacco, played
cards, told vulgar stories around the camp fires, or related their personal unlawful experiences with confiding females of good character and distrusting ones of
bad. Among these men Robbie was a general favorite,
and more than a thousand arms were ready to bear him
safely from the battlefields when danger threatened.
The reader can readily see the boy's environment was
not conducive to saintly qualities. In a year he had
scarcely seen a woman, and in the presence of one like
Phœbe, who was now so near him that his hand, lying

over the edge of the sofa, touched her dress, he felt more awe than he ever felt in the presence of a cannon. To him Phœbe was already more than a woman. She was an angel. Mentally this point was settled.

In his short life, with his experiences of the world and with all the various sensations he had known, that which pervaded his mind and reached from the ends of his toes to the roots of his hair now was different from them all. One thing he felt and knew, that he would like to be this woman's slave; like to be near enough to always touch the hem of her dress and look into those wondrous eyes. When she passed her hand over his forehead, pushed the curls out of his eyes, and asked, "How's my little drummer boy to-day?" Robbie knew he had just experienced the happiest moment of his life. He sat bolt upright, gazed intently at Phœbe a moment, then said:

"If this ain't a dream, I never felt better in my life."

"This is not a dream," said Phœbe. "I wish part of it was a dream," and a sigh escaped her as she thought of the absent brothers.

"Has the army stopped runnin' yet?" asked Robbie.

"Yes; and what a terrible battle it was. Oh, I hope this will end the war. I know my brothers are dead," and Phœbe began to cry in spite of herself.

To see this divine creature shed tears like other mortals, while it touched Robbie's heart, nevertheless did much to assure him that she was flesh and blood and an inhabitant of this earth after all. He supressed his own emotions and said:

"The war won't end, miss, till every slave is free; till every rebel is dead or surrenders."

"Thee must not call me 'miss.' "

"No?" said Robbie.

"No, my name is Phœbe. Thee must call me Phœbe, and I will call thee Robert. We use the plain language here. My father is Phineas Strong; my mother is Rachel."

"You'se must be Philadelphi Quakers, " said the boy.

"We are Virginia Quakers. I have always lived here."

"Wish I could live in a place like this. I'd be a Quaker, too!" he replied, looking around the room.

"Where is thy home?"

"Home!" The boy actually sneered it. "I have no home. Don't think I ever had a real home. Pap and mam didn't get along good. We never had nothin' like that "(pointing to the honeysuckle through the window);" no birds ever sung, no flowers ever bloomed where I lived."

"And what will become of thee now?"

"If I could get a bite to eat, miss—Phœbe, I mean— I'll try and find the army, beg Captain Barr to let me follow the regiment, get a new drum, and be in the front of the next battle. Do you know that Saturday morning, just before pap was hit, my drum was nearly full of bullets Oh! ain't them rebs dandy fighters; every fight I ve been in we ve got the worst of it. I don't say this because you'se is a rebel, but Gen'r'l Lee can just about make a monkey out of any general we've got. Pap says there is only one general in the Union army who can do these people, and before the war is over he'll be the head of the whole thing. He says somebody ought to tell Mr. Lincoln."

"Who is he?"

"I think pap said Grant—yes, Grant's his name. Pap says he can't be whipped by nobody. Oh, I'd like to fight with a gen'r'l who wouldn't be all the time ridin' along the lines, saying: 'Fall back, boys, fall back!' Why, before the battle of Malvern Hill we was all runnin' like sheep, and Hooker, fighting Joe, they called him, came along on a big black horse—it was awful hot—and says: 'Throw away your haversacks, boys,' and 'way went the haversacks. Purty soon he comes ridin' back, past me, and says, 'Let go your knapsacks, boys! throw down them colors! drop that drum, boy, and run faster, or you'll never see your mother again!'

"Then 'way went the knapsacks and down went the colors, but I kept my drum, and carried it all day in the battle of Malvern Hill, though a piece of shell cut the straps clean through, and I fell over it twice before I could get up again. Pap tho't I was a goner; told me to go to the rear an' get under a wagon, or he'd knock my head off with the flagstaff. But the fightin' then was just too beautiful, an' I says, 'Knock away, dad,' but pap didn't knock, so I stayed. We held our line all day, with nothin' to eat, and nearly dyin' with thirst, and the gen'r'ls would gallop along an' say:

'Here they come, now steady, boys, steady!' and then 'fire!' Then the smoke would go up, and you'd see the Johnnies tumblin' down the hill. I reckon I saw three thousand dead and dyin' soldiers that day!''

"Horrible!" said Phœbe. "I hope thee will never fight again! Doesn't thee know that it is wrong to fight?"

"Not in a war?"

"Yes, in a war."

"Pap said it was glory."

"Thy father's glory led him to the grave."

At this remark Robbie's throat choked up, his eyes filled, and he burst into tears, realizing for the first time, perhaps, since the awful tragedy which deprived him of a father, the loneliness and significance of his situation. Phœbe's heart was doubly touched. She put her arm around this dirty, forlorn little hero, and allowed him to cry on her bosom, as he might have done upon the breast of a mother or a sister.

In this position, half-supporting, and comforting him with gentle words, she led him from the room. With her own hands she wiped the tears away, brushed and arranged his curls, and when he was seated at the breakfast table, good, kind Rachel Strong put her arms about his soiled and brown neck, and said

"I had a little boy name Robbie, but he went to the war, and now——"

Tears came into her eyes, seeing which both Robbie and Phœbe began to cry. They were discovered in this situation by Phineas Strong, as he entered the room.

"There, there, there," he said, tenderly taking his wife and daughter in his big, strong arms, "we must not give way so. We must be brave, and try to comfort those whose misfortunes are greater than our own. My little man," turning to Robbie, "I suppose thee would like to go home to thy mother. Well, tell me where she is and I will contrive some way to get thee to her; and, mother, see if thee can't get some better clothes for him to wear."

"If you will tell me where the army is," said Robbie, "I will go there. I do not want to go home, nor do I want to see my mother. Besides I don't know where she is, and if I did I wouldn't tell!"

"Why, thou art a wicked lad, I am afraid. Not want to see thy mother; want to run away and follow the army. Child, thee needs some one to look after thee!" said Phineas.

"The boys," answered Robbie, "they'll look after me. If I can find the regiment I am all right. Just let me leave my father's knapsack here; its full of his letters and pictures. When the war is over I'll be a general, an' if you don't mind, I'll ride up to your house some day and ask for my father's things, and take them up North with me."

"My son," said Phineas, "there are plenty in the war without thee, and if thou wilt not return home, let me urge thee to remain with us until thee thinks better of my suggestion."

Phineas Strong was a student of human nature. He read Robbie's disposition, reader, like you would read a book. In his broad face and blue eyes he saw frankness and courage, and in his square chin and in his mouth he read a firmness like a rock; and while he felt like designating Robbie as a willful and obstinate boy, he inwardly knew that to this child whatever he commanded, or did, would be regarded with the most independent indifference. He might have kicked this helpless, homeless wanderer into the big road, and left him to the mercies of the war, only his own heart was as tender as a woman's and this looked to him more like a case where sympathy would accomplish more than censure. His kindly invitation to remain was what Robbie most desired, and least expected. How it was received was immediately expressed and communicated to all by the radiance that lighted up his face.

"Oh, sir!" he exclaimed, "can I really stay here? Will you—let me—let me work for you? Why, sir, I will be your slave, and do all you bid me."

Phineas had judged rightly; these few words of confidence and kindness had won the boy completely. Between these two, the old Quaker and the army arab, there instantly sprang up an esteem, each for the other, that lasted through all time.

As for Phœbe, though she could not tell why a feeling of the sweetest satisfaction stole over her as she kissed her father and said:

"Thee is always right and always good."

This, reader, is the introduction to my scenes, and to you, the hero of my story. Pardon prolixity, but all I have written seems necessarily a part of my tale.

CHAPTER X.

TRIFLING incidents alter the whole current of our lives. Phineas Strong's kind words were the beginning of a metamorphosis in the character of Robbie Porter. In three days his was a different personage. Under the influence of kindness, refinement, flowers, books, and the interest Phœbe took in him, he had become a bright and happy boy.

As my story in the future is about these two people, I will pass over the sorrowful details attending the discovery of Phineas Strong that all of his boys were killed outright in the battle of Chancellorsville, and that he was never able to recover their remains. That black George, it was learned, lost his life trying to deliver his messages to the Strong boys at Falmouth, and that a settled sorrow for many days thereafter like a dark shadow hung around River View. But as the deepest grief is often the least conspicuous, the woe of the Strongs, in a community where woe had already filled every household, was not marked by many open expressions of sympathy. The fact that the Strong boys had lost their lives fighting against the South was really a cause for withholding much that might otherwise have been given.

The Strongs were socially an isolated family. They

were regarded as a trifle peculiar. Few people came to the house, and Phœbe, although the prettiest, smartest, and I have no doubt, the best girl at that time in that part of Virginia, had no girl confidanté and no lover. She was now past twenty, and living in a community where many a girl of fourteen had half a dozen gallants at church or party. Of course all the young men were off to the war, and had been for two years, so that this may have, in a measure, accounted for Phœbe's lack of sweethearts. Yet, reader, I doubt very much, though the whole neighborhood had swarmed with handsome Southern boys, brave enough to face the cannon's mouth, there would be found one sufficiently bold to address this charming girl. Just why this was so I will not now stop to explain, for, reader, thou canst see already she had a beautiful face, a pleasing person, a tender heart, a most agreeable disposition, a bright and proper mind, and would, at some time, come into a large fortune. It would seem that at least a dozen cavaliers should nightly tie their foaming chargers to her father's gate posts. But none came a-wooing, and now that the war would undoubtedly kill the handsomest and the bravest, Phœbe's matrimonial chances were improving about as rapidly as the Southern Confederacy was declining.

Between you and me, reader, I do not think Phœbe ever troubled herself very much about the peculiar conditions which surrounded her. At the opening of my story she seemed, so far as Cupid's arts prevailed, heart whole and fancy free, and having never had or lost a

lover, never sighed for one. She was therefore happy
—that is, as happy as a good, pure, innocent girl, in
the bloom of health and flush of womanhood, whose
every temporal want is supplied, and whose knowledge
of the world is limited to its goodness, could possibly be.

Thus far her life had been without incident or accident. She had been educated at home, had never been
further away than Fredericksburg, and never, to her
knowledge, had seen a steamboat, or ridden in a railway
coach. She rode a horse, however, my fair reader,
much more gracefully than you ride "a wheel," and I
have no doubt she would have been inexpressibly
shocked had she thought, in doing so, it was necessary
to display the symmetry of her legs so as to excite the
envy of other horsewomen. She had never seen a piano
or witnessed a theatrical performance. She was indeed a combination of ignorance and innocence, the
types of which have long since vanished from the
earth. Her knowledge of books was limited to "Uncle
Tom's Cabin," "Isaac Tatum Hopper," "The Pilgrim's Progress," "Queechie" and "Jane Eyre."
The only newspapers at which she ever looked were
The Friends' Intelligencer, and the New York
Tribune. She seldom ever read either of them. But,
reader, she could make the sweetest butter that ever
came from cream, and the lightest rolls and biscuits to
go with it that ever came from oven. She could also
crochet, spin flax, and knit socks and mittens. With
the needle she was quite an artist, and had filled the
house with fancy work. Her gowns and bonnets were.

her own handiwork, but as they always conformed to
the styles affected by the religious sect to which she
belonged, she had little opportunity in this respect to
display any variety in taste.

The striking quality about the Strongs was industry,
and while there was always a dozen or more black
people about, Phineas Strong gave his personal attention to all of the outside labor, while Phœbe and her
mother found in the house ample opportunities to display and practice those domestic arts which made this
home the most comfortable and attractive in all the
country.

The smoke house was always full of sweet hams;
rows of jars, filled with preserved fruits adorned many
long shelves.   The attic was always stuffed with herbs,
such as sage, old man, thyme, mint, snakeroot, mul-
berry leaves, hops, walnuts, hickory nuts, chestnuts,
shellbark, chincapins, dried fruits and flaxseed.   The
hand of plenty in this house was forever open, and this
suggestion came to you first on sitting down in the spacious dining room.   All of this was such a striking
contrast to Robbie's former life, he a long while
doubted its reality, and expected every morning to
wake up and find himself sheltered by a dirty canvas
tent, or, perhaps, completely exposed to the stars of
heaven and the damp dews of the night.

He had been here a week now, and had not heard an
oath or a cross word; he had been in the army two
years and heard nothing else.   Everybody was kind.
There was not a whip or rod on the entire estate.   He

learned that even the cattle and horses were never whipped. At house or barn the doors were never locked, day or night, and often not even closed. Money was allowed to be exposed to the view of all, and was apparently regarded with less care than any other article of value in the house. At night there was no locking of drawers, no bolting of doors, no fastening of windows. The family retired to rest with a feeling of confidence that could never have been the product of anything but virtue and serenity.

Robbie was something of a philosopher, and in a little while adapted himself to the situation. His disposition being naturally a genial one, and his temper obliging, it was not long before he was a general favorite with the whole household. He was, in fact, a brave and generous little man. He was deeply grateful, and consequently always willing. He soon became such a necessity that his departure was no longer talked about, and as he continued in his refusal to disclose his mother's address, the subject at last became too remote for casual revival. Robbie Porter was a fixture in the Strong household. He was treated like a son and a brother. His ragged regimentals, with his father's old pistol and his knapsack, had been consigned to the attic along with last year's herbs and seeds; and, I am sorry to write it, the memories of both were fast fading from his mind.

The griefs of the young are short lived, and his new life, tender, solicitous surroundings, gradually but surely dissipated the recollections of his former miserable experiences and bloody exhibitions.

I have ever been of the opinion that a proper influence, either in man, woman, or child, in plant or animal life, will develop the better qualities of all. A more marked illustration of this truth could not be cited than in the case of my hero. His good qualities, heretofore stunted or dormant, began to expand, and were soon thoroughly apparent to his benefactors. Bravery, frankness, generosity, and a highly receptive mind, it was soon seen he possessed to a marked degree. These qualities, in the minds of the Strongs, were essentials. In a few months they and the servants all wondered how it was they ever got along without Robbie Porter.

CHAPTER XI.

TOWARD our little waif of the war, Phœbe began immediately to display the tender affection of a sister and exercise the solicitude of a mother. To her ho had already become the bravest and brightest little character of which she had ever heard. In fiction, she thought, had she ever had the opportunity to ramble in its charming realms, there might have been such a personage as our hero, but certainly not in real life. From his stories of battle experiences Phœbe was convinced that her *protégé* possessed a physical courage that amounted to absolute fearlessness. This quality will win a man homage in camp or court, and to the female mind is the most potent charm the opposite sex can possess. It was not then very surprising, that my backwoods, country-born heroine formed for Robbie an admiration which she seemed proud not to conceal.

In a hundred little ways Phœbe made manifest to all her affection. She deemed it her especial business to look after his wardrobe. She purchased his hats, his shoes, made his shirts, his coats, his trousers, knit his socks and mittens, brushed or combed his hair in the morning; lighted him to bed at night, tucked him in, as a mother would, and kissed him good-night as freely and unreservedly as a sister. Once a week, seventh

day evenings, in the summer she sent him to the river
with soap and towels, with positive instructions to
bathe all over, and, if when he returned, she found
after inspection he had missed his ears, or a part of his
neck, as a boy sometimes will, she took cloth and soap
and completed the ablutions.

She brought forth from the attic, all of her brothers'
school books, and a few miscellaneous volumes, which
included "The Boy's Book of Adventures," Goldsmith's "Animated Nature," Irving's "Life of Washington," Goodrich's "History of the United States,"
and two venerable volumes of "Shakespeare," edited by
Johnson. These were all at Robbie's disposal, and all
of his spare time, aside from his daily tasks, was spent
in their perusal.

Phœbe tried constantly to stimulate him to study,
and assigned him lessons which he recited to her
nightly. His readings and studies soon made manifest a quality heretofore unnoticed. This was a prodi-
gious memory. It was apparent that study was a mere
pastime; that he had only to glance at a page in a
book and then repeat it word for word. He could read
fifteen or twenty pages of his history, close the volume,
or allow Phœbe to hold it, and repeat it without a
single mistake. It was but a little while before he had
read every book in the house, and knew their contents
by heart. The plays of "Shakespeare" and their characters he had at his tongue's end, and was continually
repeating passages and even pages from them.

Just what impression the scenes in "Juliet" and

some of the lines in "Venus and Adonis," and the "Rape of Lucrece" had upon the mind of a boy of thirteen I will not pretend to say, but Robbie mentally sometimes wished that he was back in the army, that he might tell the boys all about them.

In justice to the Strongs, however, especially to Phœbe and her mother, they had no more idea of the contents of some of these volumes than they had of the Talmud. Their tastes being exclusively directed to those domestic duties which are the charm and virtue of the good housewife, books and their contents were regarded as frivolous. Of the great world of letters these good people had no conception. "Knowledge to their eyes her ample page rich with the spoils of time did ne'er unroll," and to get the gooseberry jam just right was of more consequence to them than a whole page of poetry, with a recitation of which Robbie would sometimes try to entertain them.

To his reading, therefore, the boy was left without guidance or direction, and had he found in the house Fielding, Rabelais, Byron or Morte d'Arthur he would have perused them without restraint. Of the advancement of her pupil, Phœbe was immensely proud. His feats of memory astonished and delighted her. She encouraged him in every possible way to read and study; ransacked the house for books for him; and one day from some mysterious and remote corner of that old attic brought forth Harkness' first Latin book, a Latin grammar, a Latin reader, a Latin dictionary, Cæsar's Commentaries, a copy of Sallust's "Jugurthine

War," and Virgil's "Æneid" Without stopping to examine them, she carried them all to Robbie, and delightedly laid them before him. Their disappointment was mutual and touching when an extended examination disclosed the fact that not one sentence in any of them could he read.

Of all of these little kindnesses Robbie was not only sensible but deeply grateful. His pride, however, was humiliated at the thought of his dependence. In return for this goodness crowded upon him, there was, it seemed, so little that he could do. To work each day in the field or garden, to help his uncle (for so he called Phineas Strong), about the barns, to assist Aunt Rachel in little things about the house, and to help Phœbe with the butter, to bring in the eggs, and run errands, were, in his mind, not even worthy the board and clothes he received. At times the reflection that he was a child of charity forced itself upon him. Yet, he thought, he would rather be a slave than be asked to leave.

For Phœbe he had conceived an affection, which, though he realized it not then, was destined to last forever. In her presence he was always happy, and he never left her side without emotions of regret, and never returned to her presence without the keenest sensations of joy. Night and day, in his work in the field, in his dreams, Phœbe's face was before him. To him there was but one beautiful and glorious being in all the world, and that was Phœbe. His devotion to her was as marked as it was constant. Not a day passed but he made manifest to all that she was the delight of his youthful attention, and the chief object of his boyish gallantry.

If, wandering in the woods, he found a bunch of berries redder and more luscious than all the rest, he saved them with a tender and jealous care, and presented them to Phœbe. If upon a remote and perilous limb of the ox-heart cherry tree there dangled a bunch of fruit more solid and more perfect than all the rest, he valiantly risked his life that he might pluck and lay it in Phœbe's lap. If upon the Crawford peach tree there hung over the garden wall a peach riper and rosier than the others, larger, and blushing its glory in the sun, he quickly scaled the wall and stopped nor stayed not till that same peach was fondled in Phœbe's hand. The largest and reddest apple in the orchard found its way to Phœbe. The wild flowers of the wood and the cultivated posies of the garden were always in Phœbe's vases. If he caught a fine trout in the river, he carried it to Phœbe; if, in hunting in the wood with old Sam, the colored Nimrod of the place, he shot a squirrel or bird, they were seen to be laid at Phœbe's feet.

If Phœbe rode out he rode by her side. He gallantly pushed the overhanging branches of the trees from her face, and quickly refastened her saddle girth if it parted. He was quick to assist her to alight, and dextrous in helping her to remount. He could take her little foot in his hand and reseat her in the saddle with the certainty and grace of a cavalier. If she wished to cross the river, Robbie rowed the boat, and sometimes, I verily believe, he wished she would fall overboard so he could jump in and rescue her. He never doubted for a moment that he could do this, although Phœbe weighed one hundred and thirty pounds. He would often wish something would happen so he could show her how grateful he was. Often, when riding with her through the woods, he hoped some brute of a soldier would suddenly appear and insult her. Then he would show her how soon he would kill the villain. Indeed he hoped that some time Phœbe would ask him to cut out his heart; he had resolved to show her how very quickly he would comply with her request.

But none of these things ever happened. There was much of sameness in the lives of these two people. The war for awhile raged around them, and they daily met and fed weak and wandering fugitives of both armies. Nothing, however, molested these quiet people. The great conflict ended very much as Robbie once predicted. That combination of Napoleon and Wellington, Ulysses S. Grant, succeeded in destroying most of the Confederate forces, and in surrounding the balance, so that even the brilliant resources of Lee were no longer available. The war ceased. Virginia, among the last to secede, was among the first to return to the Union.

From the standpoint of glory the war was a grand success. In all other respects it was a miserable and expensive failure. Perhaps the unprejudiced student of history will conclude, as I have, that the greater glory

was with the South, because it opposed with six hundred thousand soldiers an army of three million.
However, had the war never occurred my story had
never been written.

Peace, which in the vicinity of River View had
really never been much disturbed, prevailed in all the
country. The vanquished, such as were yet alive, returned to their depleted and ruined homes. Most of
Phineas Strong's old neighbors, broken in hearts, helpless, nearly homeless, came back, and resignedly tried
to make the best of the situation.

There was Colonel Wren, Captain Edwards, Major
Fields, "Cat" Doggett, Henry Turner and others,
whom he knew as good, noble men. He saw them
ride away, proud, haughty, rich, flushed with health,
and buoyant with hope. Many of them, like himself,
had lost sons, but all had lost what wealth they once
possessed. Most of these men were now old and gray,
and some of them walked home—that is, to where
home once was.

None of these men had been long from the last battlefield before they were visited by Phineas Strong. He
did not go to gloat over their failure. No, he took saddle bags full of money, and to each one said:

"Friend, thou hast suffered many hardships, and thy
affairs are in bad shape. I have brought my purse, and
such sums as thou needest I will cheerfully advance
for an indefinite time without interest." And to each
one he passed the saddle bags.

Henry Fields was too proud to accept. "Cat" Doggett, who had not a hoof on his farm, said: "You can't, you don't mean it! Why, sir, we killed your boys! do you know that?"

"I don't think thee killed them, Cataline. Besides, thee has a wife and children alive. Thee will need money to help thee take care of them. If thou wilt not take the money, come over and get a team and a cow and feed for them till thee can raise a crop."

Doggett took the old man's hands in his own, burst into tears and said:

"Sir, we can never forget your kindness. You have saved me!"

To the widow Kemper, whose husband had been killed at Cold Harbor, and who was left with four daughters, Phineas sent a horse and one of his hired help, and food enough to supply them for a year.

Most of Strong's neighbors availed themselves of his kindness; and in a few months that section of Virginia was blooming and blossoming as though the ravages of war had never devastated it.

After such an exhibition of generosity, it would have been a cold and unfeeling community that saw nothing in the character of Phineas Strong to admire. Indeed, the whole neighborhood softened toward him. His eccentricities were forgotten, and his virtues lauded by every tongue. Every eye regarded him with admiration, and every hand from the tiniest babe to the venerable veteran was inspired to applaud his name. The social barriers, which for more than twenty years had grown around this noble family, were suddenly destroyed, and the descendants of Lord Fairfax vied with each other in showering attentions and homage upon these innocent and modest objects of their esteem.

Of all the young ladies in the neighborhood, Miss Phœbe was now allowed by all the men to be the most beautiful, most charming and most modest, and, I am happy to inform my readers, in most cases, their wives and daughters assented.

Robbie was now fifteen. In two years he had grown taller and broader.

As the escort of Phœbe he frequently attended the "husking bees," "apple parings," and "choppings," or "log rollings," that furnished the chief sources of social entertainment at that time, and perhaps do yet. · At these social functions, after the work of the day and the feast concluded, a violin was produced, and the crowd of harmless boys and blushing girls "lead up the dance," till the "we sma' hours."

Quakers never dance; they look upon the art with disfavor, and at these parties our pretty Phœbe, had she been contesting for high social recognition, would have entered the lists somewhat handicapped. All entreaties, however, to get her to participate in those simple evolutions required by "Money musk," and "Virginia reel" failed. Beautiful and blushing, happy and modest, she sat, content to follow Robbie's form around the room as he danced his feet sore with some giggling stripling who would be so tickled at his gallantry that she was compelled to bite her lips to keep from exploding her pride.

Having participated in several affairs of this kind, Phœbe had prevailed upon her mother to give an "apple paring." To it were invited most of the families with whom the Strongs were acquainted; and, forgetting that the Strongs were Yankees, nearly everybody came. The apples were pared, and the apple butter stirred a little by everybody present. An ample feast was spread and destroyed, when Sam Bunch, whose reputation with the fiddle was far ahead of that of Orpheus, especially in Culpepper County, produced his instrument and shouted: "All take your places for a plain quadrille!"

Many expected Phineas Strong would enter a protest. He did nothing of the kind. The man's natural goodness was such that he really encouraged them to proceed.

Robbie, who had often begged Phœbe to try a dance with him, finding that his uncle did not frown upon the proposed entertainment, hastened to her side, and, though she had just refused Colonel Wren, the handsomest and most distinguished guest present, suffered Robbie to lead her to the position of *vis-à-vis* to the first couple. Phœbe's natural grace of motion carried her not only successfully but admiringly through the entire dance; and blushing as she never before blushed in her whole life, at its conclusion, clinging to Robbie's arm, radiant and happy, took her seat and soon had twenty offers to dance the next "set."

Now, reader, I could no more fathom a woman's mind than I could calculate an eclipse. Phœbe's face diffused a glory that only the happiest heart could reflect, yet—must I write it?—she persistently refused to dance with any of her admirers. Robbie had whirled away with Dora Kemper, a miss of fourteen, with a superb little form, and a pair of black eyes that were calculated to make mischief with any heart. Whether Miss Dora squeezed Robbie's hand in the grand "rights" and "lefts" more firmly than some of the others, I know not; but whatever the reason, it will never be known, so let us be content with the fact that Dora and Robbie danced oftener together than any other couple.

Betty Turner, a budding blonde of sixteen, who could scarcely keep her eyes off of Robbie's brown curls, was heard to remark to Ella Wren: "I do think that Dora Kemper is just too bold for anything!"

At which the simpering Ella simpered more, but in the least possible consoling way to the ruffled Betty.

The widow Kemper, with her four daughters, was present, and at two o'clock in the morning, when it was time to depart, it was found all had secured escorts but Dora. This, accidentally, of course, was not discovered by the fair Dora until her mother and sisters, with their escorts, had already taken their departure. The gallant Robbie, however, seeing in this a fortuitous opportunity, flew to the rescue. Without so much as a demur he obtained from the little designer prompt permission to see her home. His heart fairly jumped at the prospect. He soon had Dora behind him on one of his uncle's best horses, and, prouder than he was the day he beat a tattoo at Malvern Hill, proceeded four miles through a dark woods to deliver his lovely charge into the arms of her anxious mother.

Reader, didst ever take a young lady behind thee on a horse through a dark woods at two o'clock in the morning from a country dance? If thou hast never done this, then thou hast lived a tame and tasteless life. Joys, pleasures, delights, sensations, sweetnesses, all different from anything you have ever known, or will know, flood you during that experience. How you wish the evening was just beginning, that the road was a couple of hundred miles long, and that the darkness was darker, and—that you could turn around without twisting your head off—(the inability to turn around is really quite a drawback to the complete success of a ride like this). In this particular ride, Miss Dora, who could "set" a horse as easily as most girls occupy a chair, and far more gracefully, for some reason or other, came so near falling off that she really was compelled to pass her arms under Robbie's and clasp him firmly about the waist.

In this way, and in this way alone, was she able to maintain her equilibrium. Thus the pair safely arrived in front of her mother's door, where the fair burden gracefully slipped to the horse block. What these two talked during the ride, the bliss of which I doubt if either ever forgot, I cannot tell. I did not hear it. Robbie galloped home, and walking into the still lighted dining room, was somewhat surprised to find Phœbe waiting for him.

CHAPTER XII.

If my readers imagine I am going to advance any conclusions as to this interview between a robust lad of fifteen and a beautiful girl of twenty-two, alone, in a big room, of a big house, at four o'clock in the morning, they will be mistaken. I conceive it the duty of an historian to relate facts, and to the imagination of his auditors leave the task of philosophical speculation. Therefore I propose to relate this little scene just as it occurred.

Phœbe, who had occupied a quaint, rush-bottomed chair, and was gazing, rather pensively to be sure, upon the crackling embers of a fading fire on the hearth as Robbie entered, suddenly arose, went directly to meet him, gave him a most tender and melting glance, which he neither understood nor appreciated, and taking his hand in one of hers and his hat in the other, said:

"Why, Robbie, thee is quite a gallant," And without waiting for a reply continued: "Come, sit down and tell me all that thee and Dora talked about on the way home;" and she led him to the little rocker.

Robbie sat down, reached over for the bootjack that reclined against the chimney jam, and proceeded to pull his feet out of his top boots.

"Thee wants to tease me. Thee doesn't care to know," said Robbie.

She leaned over his shoulder behind, brushed her cheek against his, swept a curl from his forehead with her hand, and answered: "I sat up on purpose to have thee tell me. Please tell me all that *she* said and all that *thee* said."

There was an earnestness in her tone that left no doubt in Robbie's mind that Phœbe was terribly sincere. Her right to question him he never doubted. He saw, or thought he saw, that if he would relate the little *tête-à-téte* between him and Dora it would give Phœbe pleasure, and if he ever in his life wanted to confer happiness upon any human being it was upon Phœbe Strong. Without, therefore, the remotest idea of any purpose other than delighting her he said:

"Well, Phœbe, to please thee and amuse thee, I'll tell thee all that I can remember."

"If thee tells me all thee can remember," said Phœbe, "thee will not miss much."

"Well," said Robbie.

"Well," said Phœbe.

"Well, let me see—well, thee knows just as we got through the gate at the Ford road, she came near falling off, and——"

"And what?" asked Phœbe.

"Why, well, thee knows she had to throw her arms around me to save herself."

"And did she?"

"Why, of course—and then, thee knows how dark it

was—well, when Dora had recovered her balance she said—said——"

"Said what?" queried Phœbe.

"Why, she said it was so dark, and sne was so little, she reckoned if she did fall off I couldn't find her, so she said it was safer maybe, it was so dark for her to—to——"

"To what?"

"To hold on that way till we got home."

"The bold little vixen," said Phœbe, as she allowed her arm to fall fondly about Robbie's shoulder.

"Yes, that's what I thought," said Robbie.

"And what else did she say?"

"Oh, she chattered right along—did most of the talking."

"Tell me what she said!"

"She said a mighty lot!"

"What?"

"Oh, she leaned her face to one side against my shoulder, and said—said: 'It's just as natural for boys and girls to love one another as it is for grown people, don't you think so, Master Porter?' "

"What a bold little girl," said Phœbe.

"Yes," went on Robbie, "that's what I thought."

"Well?"

"Well, that's about all, I guess!"

"Oh, no, it isn't; thee must have said something to her!"

"Well, I thought I did, but blessed if I can think now what I did say!"

"No?"

"No! but she said I should come over Sunday—First day evening—and take tea with her ma."

"With her mother?"

"Yes, that's what she said, but she said she would be at home too, and 'we all' would have a nice time."

"The little designer," said Phœbe, as she disengaged her arm. "And did thee tell her thee would come?"

"Yes, that's what I promised."

"Promised?"

"Yes, she made me promise for sure, because she said it would be very disappointin' and annoyin' to her ma if I didn't come."

Phœbe took the candle from the chimney piece, snuffed it, looked up into Robbie's face; he was standing now, and taller than she, and said:

"Robbie, I don't think father would like thee to visit the Kempers. Promise me on his account thee will not go there First day evening."

This was a great thing to exact of Robbie, because Dora had made deep inroads into his heart already and he had pictured that coming First day evening's tea with her in the most lively colorings a bright and hopeful imagination could portray.

"Why, if thee doesn't want me to go, Phœbe, of course, thee knows I wouldn't think of it."

"I am sure I don't, because there are better families in the neighborhood than the Kempers, and father— would like to see thee associate with only the best."

"All right," said Robbie, "I promise thee not to go."

"Good-night," she said, handing him the candle, "I am going to Fredericksburg to-morrow, and if thee is up in time I will get father to let thee ride with me." With that she disappeared through a doorway, forgetting, as usual, perhaps, to kiss her *protégé*, as she had done nightly since his advent into the house. Whether on this occasion she really forgot, I know not, but she never renewed the custom.

Phœbe, having retired to her own room, and Robbie to his in the attic, and it being now nearly daybreak, I will defer till another time detailing the reflections of either occasioned by the scene I have just described.

CHAPTER XIII.

A LATE retiring induces a late arising. Exhausted nature required of Robbie a long rest, and when he awoke, the sun was already past the meridian. Phœbe, he soon learned, had hours before set out for Fredericksburg, and must now be well on her way toward home. He was proceeding to saddle a horse with the purpose of going to meet her, when from a box stall adjoining where he stood he heard Phineas Strong say:

"Sam, thee better take the colt and kill it, too. The poor thing will be better off."

To scale the board partition that divided him from the voice was so easy that in an instant Robbie stood in the box stall beside his uncle and in the midst of a half-dozen servants.

A look showed him the dead and mangled body of one of his uncle's finest and most costly brood mares. The poor thing, lacking natural force necessary to bring her offspring into the world, had perished, a victim to the surgeon's knife, and her helpless little baby, dragged into the light, lay in a shapeless mass against her upturned flanks.

"Please, uncle," said Robbie piteously, bending down to look at the little colt, "please don't kill it.

Give it to me. Please, uncle, do. I will take care of it. Won't thee, Uncle Phineas?"

The boy was kneeling in the straw, and beseechingly looking into the face of the kind-hearted Quaker.

Phineas, while he felt it would have been a humane act to allow Sam to execute his order, seeing how earnest Robbie was, and loving him already to a degree that he was quite unwilling to admit, even to himself, said: "Well, Sam, let Robbie have the colt; but hurry up and bury the mare."

"Oh, thank thee, uncle, thank thee; and it's mine, isn't it?"

"Yes," said Phineas; "but thee must raise it thyself."

"Oh, I'll raise it," said Robbie, as he proceeded immediately to wrap it in a blanket; and then, before any were aware of his purpose, he took the limp and almost inanimate mass in his arms, and bore it to the house, where, without leave or license, he deposited it on the floor in front of that same fireplace where he and Phœbe had talked on his return from Dora Kemper.

Just here at this time his gratitude for the kindness of Phineas Strong prompted him to make a mental wish that he might never see the face of Dora Kemper again.

When Phœbe entered the room an hour later she found him holding the colt's head in his lap, and feeding it warm milk from a bottle.

How this dumb, motherless thing appealed to Robbie. Its helpless condition awakened all of the tender impulses of his warm heart. He watched over it with a solicitude as touching as constant. For two nights he slept on the floor by its side. He fed it, patted it, groomed it, cleaned it, and at last had the satisfaction and joy of seeing it stand upon its feet. He then led it forth to the open day, and even the November sunbeams infused it with energy and life.

And now Robbie owned a colt. There was one thing on the generous earth that was really his; his because he earned it; his because he saved it. How proud to think that he was the actual, undisputed possessor of this one piece of property.

The complete realization of this great fact enabled him within a week after the event to examine the books Phœbe had brought him from Fredericksburg. Among them were the then complete poems of Henry W. Longfellow, Macaulay's "History of England," and "Norwood," a novel by Henry Ward Beecher, just out, all of which Robbie eagerly devoured.

And here, perhaps as well as at any other time, I will ask the reader's pardon for failing to detail Phœbe's reflections on the morning after her talk with Robbie about Dora Kemper. Now the fact is, from the circumstances I could only conjecture what those reflections were. Reader, thou canst also conjecture.

Again permit me, ere I conclude this chapter, to apologize for making so much of the birth of a colt. But the fact is the colt from this time, and for a considerable period, becomes one of the most important personages of my story. It was one of the circumstances flung around the life of Robert Porter which changed its whole course, and in the end separated him from, and robbed him of, the only being in his life that filled all the interstices of his heart and absorbed all of his generous affection.

CHAPTER XIV.

READER, didst ever upon some dumb animal lavish the fond and unselfish love of a young and buoyant heart? Didst ever with thy faithful dog share the last crust, or with thy noble steed on the tented field of battle divide thy hard-tack and thy sugar? If not, thou canst not conceive the affection Robbie formed for this ill-starred colt. She (for such was the sex) became his daily companion. She knew his voice, and whinnied her joy at the approach of his form; and Robbie, barring Phœbe, of course, regarded her as the most priceless object in the universe.

Somewhere in this story the reader will remember Phœbe had resuscitated from the gloom of the garret some Latin volumes formerly belonging to her dead brothers. Having read and re-read every book in the house but these, Robbie had, at Phœbe's suggestion, undertaken to decipher their contents. So that, when the winter had passed, he was already through the Latin reader. Thinking the "Æneid" more to his taste than the war in Gaul, he boldly started with "Arma Virumque cano," etc., and soon was completely carried away by the charm and pathos of this matchless epic.

The interest in the story grew so absorbing that he found its reading more of a pleasure than a task. In

the stillness of the night, when the world around him
slumbered, diligently he dug out the melancholy story
of the fall of Troy, and the heart-touching fate of the
distracted Dido. Sweet and plaintive drama! It expanded his dawning mind and swelled his awakening
soul!

With what tender interest had he followed Æneas
in his search for the Golden Apple; and with what
wide-eyed wonder had he gone with him in all of his
weary wanderings through the realms of hell. How,
in the summer evenings, lulled by the distant murmurs
of the rolling river and fanned by those perfumed and
gentle breezes that exhale the aroma of the pine, and
the flavor of the dogwood blossom, he would sit down
at the feet of Phœbe, even perhaps as Glaucus reclined
before the beauteous Ione, and tell her the story of the
noble Æneas and the sad, sad death of his unhappy
mistress of Carthage.

By this time his pet colt had become strong and graceful, but of such a nondescript color that no one had as
yet ever seen anything like it. Her legs were of a yel-
lowish hue, and her body something of a mouse color,
mixed with gray, the gray hairs being apparently
longer than the others and covering her entire body
so as to give her the appearance of being always covered with frost or wet with dew. However, her legs
were extremely long, her body slender but well proportioned, and her large head always in the air when she
moved. Her gait was invariably the trot, and often
when Robbie called her from a distance she trotted to

him with such amazing swiftness that she seemed to fly through the air like a bird. It was this quality and the peculiar color, or colors, that suggested to Robbie an appropriate name for his pet, as he had heretofore called her. He recalled from his Virgil, in that passage describing the death of the despairing Dido, how dewy Iris, with her saffron-colored wings, drawing a thousand colors from the opposite sun, flew down from heaven, and released to Pluto's place the struggling soul of the wretched woman.

So he said to Phœbe: "I will name her Dewy Iris. Her saffron legs are her wings, and while she can't fly down from heaven, some day she'll fly up from earth, and all the world will wonder!"

So this colt was known as Dewy Iris, and was afterward registered under that name in Wallace's Stud Book, where, my curious reader, if you have time and inclination, you may investigate the record of her performances on the turf, without waiting to discover them through the slow process of my tedious pages.

CHAPTER XV.

No doubt, reader, you have long since come to the conclusion that this is only a story after all. That there never was a character like Phœbe or a colt like Dewy Iris. True it is that this is a story, but, unlike most stories, is true. In this I claim a great difference exists between my book and most others. It is, therefore, my duty, and I trust your pleasure, that I proceed as rapidly as good taste will allow to relate, clearly, concisely and correctly what further befell the hero and heroine of my tale.

I propose, however, with the license of a novelist, though I am sure the public will acquit me of the charge of being one, to carry my reader forward at least four years, or until about the first of November, 1869.

I have two very cogent reasons for this. First, the intervening time had really, by fate or fortune, been allowed to pass without other than the commonplace incidents liable to happen to people living in affluence in a rich and rural district. Around the Strong household peace and plenty still extended their blessings. In the confidence of all of his fellow-beings, Phineas Strong was rounding out a life replete with goodness and perfect in results. His good wife, Rachel, calm, serene, meek, beaming in face and sweet in manner, was the idol of young and old. Phœbe, now nearly twenty-seven, was plumper and rosier, too. But, fair lady reader, she was still unmarried. What a pity! Surely all the single men in the counties of Culpepper, Stafford and Fauquier were blind.

Robbie was taller, broader and was about the handsomest young man of nineteen in the whole country. He was, too, according to all the young ladies, the bravest and brightest.

My second reason is, I will the sooner be able to entertain my readers with the more stirring incidents of my narrative. However, despite the critics, I am going to tell this story in my own way, and just as it is.

On the surface—that is, to the casual observer—all was fair as a summer's day among the occupants of River View, but I will acquaint you now with the fact that there were two members of this household that were neither perfectly happy nor serenely content. Phœbe, ever since the night she learned Dora Kemper had hugged Robbie Porter those four miles through the dark woods, had discovered an attachment for her *protégé* that was neither sisterly nor motherly. Dost think it strange that a modest, sensible, properly raised young lady of twenty-seven, a demure and discreet Quakeress, too, should be desperately in love with a lad of nineteen? If thou dost think it strange, thou must then confess truth stranger than fiction.

Phœbe had half-suspected it before the incident referred to, but the tugging around her heart when Rob-

bie related his innocent experience confirmed her sus-
picions completely.

Reluctantly, almost shamefully, she confessed to herself that she loved this boy. And what did she do?
Did she tell him? No, indeed! She set diligently to
work to repress her feelings and conceal her love. She
buried it deep down in her heart, but her natural tenderness would resuscitate it daily, call it back to
momentary memories, and then mercilessly re-inter it
in the darkest corner of that organ, where she fondly,
and in truth, concealed it from every eye but her own.
But love, like a budding blossom, will sooner or later
break from its cerements, and spreading into perfect
petals and beauteous colorings charm some nostril with
its sweet perfume.

But I must confess that I am now unable to account
for the fact that Robbie was wholly insensible, apparently, to the beauty and flavor of this rare flower that
bloomed continually about him. True, in word and
action Phœbe completely repressed all of those natural
yearnings and impulses of her heart, but in a thousand
little things, in ten thousand glowing glances, any one
not deaf, dumb and blind would have discovered that
Robbie Porter was this woman's idol.

Her training, her womanly instincts, the traditions
of her sex, the customs of her country, her own natural
delicacy, and the inborn desire of every girl to be won
and wooed, all operated as powerful agencies to impel
the continuation of her attitude toward him. Sweetly
she hoped then, and painfully she doubted, so that her

passion became at once the joy of her days and the sorrow of her silent nights.

I said that Robbie was insensible to Phœbe's charms. This really does the boy an injustice; his eyes failed to discover the condition Phœbe so artfully concealed. When a woman wants to conceal a thing she can deceive a wily, worldly man, much more easily an innocent, inexperienced boy.

But as a matter of fact, Robbie had given to Phœbe the first time he saw her face all of his boyish, ardent affection. The seven years he had associated with her had really intensified his passion. Now, nearly a man, he knew he loved her as never man loved woman. There was no sacrifice he would not have made for her. He would have been glad to stem the swiftest current to save her life; to kill the man who dared insult her; to give his heart's blood, if drinking it would quench her thirst; to face a thousand open cannons or breast as many shining sabers. But, Great God! reader! to ask her to marry him, to tell her that he loved her, were things from the contemplation of doing he quailed as a coward on the eve of battle.

Who was he, from whom this divine and perfect creature should condescend to receive the homage of love? Why, he knew of a dozen suitors who had tried to pay their addresses to her, and who had all been coldly and finally dismissed.

"None of them," thought Robbie, "were good enough for her! and—well, what do you suppose she would say to me? Laugh, and call me a foolish boy. And then," he thought, "Uncle Phineas would tell me to leave the place."

And this is just exactly what he had made up his mind to do.

To him, Phœbe Strong was a star, shining in the heavens; as a star he could gaze upon her there, but he could never reach her. He would go forth, conquer the world, build a Jacob's Ladder, ascend to that heaven where his Phœbe sparkled in her scintillating sweetness, pluck from its orbit this beauteous, burning diadem, and bear it with him to earth where it would be a lasting light in his life, never to go out, till his own perished in eternal gloom.

CHAPTER XVI.

GREAT thought, Robbie! Noble purpose! And I honor you for them both.

But you big, lubbering, sentimental clown, don't you know that your brown curls, blue eyes, broad shoulders and brave heart had made an impression on Phœbe Strong that neither time nor sorrow were ever to efface! Don't you know that at this very minute you could have walked over to her side, taken her in your big, strong arms and said, "Phœbe, I love thee, God knows I love thee; be my wife!" That she would have melted on your bosom; that Phineas Strong would have been the proudest man in all Virginia, and would have made you his heir before the sun went down behind the woods; that good Aunt Rachel would have wept upon your vacant shoulder, and blessed you with the fervor of a mother's love. You did not know these things, did you? And so, hot-headed, proud, a dreamer, you proceeded deliberately to make a fool of yourself, and by withdrawing yourself from your love, to fondly imagine you were getting nearer. Therefore, on this particular November morning, the breakfast concluded, Robbie said:

"Uncle Phineas, does Dewy Iris belong to me?"

"Why, of course; why does thee ask?"

"Well, thee knows after I entered her in the Culpepper Races last month thee forbade me to trot her, though I am sure I could have taken first money in the 2:30 class."

"Well, yes; but thee knows I am opposed to horse racing, and only requested thee not to race. Thee knows I offered thee the two hundred dollars thee might have won."

"Well," said Robbie, evidently unmindful of this noble act of his uncle, "if she is mine, I am going to ride away on her to-morrow morning, and when I come back I'll be a great man and have a dozen horses!"

Everybody rose from the table, and Phœbe disappeared. Poor Phœbe! She knew Robbie's character too well to soothe her agitation with the reflection that this was a joke. Like most young men of his age, Robbie was very "set" in his determination to carry out any scheme he might form. He had read enough, and been flattered until in his own mind he krew more than all of those about him; and Phœbe, to whom frequently of late he had communicated his intention to leave the country, was fully satisfied that he was about to put his purpose into execution.

Phineas Strong, too, was well aware of this headstrong quality in Robbie's character. He had seen it displayed in all of the boy's undertakings. He knew to expostulate, dissuade, or entreat would be an idle waste of words. He could command or employ physical force, but he knew that these, in the end, would be not only unavailing, but would stir up in Robbie a bitterness that might rupture their friendship. His own knowledge, too, of the world, enabled him in a measure to understand and appreciate the boy's desire to go away from home. He had done the same thing long before he was nineteen. Recovering, therefore, his usual calm exterior, his fairness and generosity prompted him thus:

"Robert, this is a foolish and very unnecessary purpose. Thou art, I see, however, fully persuaded to depart. May thee never regret it. Consider always this as thy home, and return freely when the spirit moves thee so to do. Dewy Iris is thine absolutely, and here," taking a roll of bank bills from a large red wallet, "are the two hundred dollars I know thee would have won had thee driven in that race."

He laid the money on the table and started from the room. Robbie caught his hand, and choking with an emotion he never before felt, said: "Uncle Phineas, thee is the best man that ever lived!"

"Thou hast seen but few men," was Phineas' reply, and walked away.

Robbie was alone with his roll of bills.

CHAPTER XVII.

GATHERING the scattered notes into a bunch, Robbie placed them carefully in his trousers' pocket, took his hat, and straightway proceeded to the barn, where, to Dewy Iris, his arms about her neck, he communicated his good fortune and brilliant prospects.

"We'll go away together, won't we, old girl?" he said, patting her affectionately. "We'll astonish the world, we will! We'll win in a race in a 2:10 clip, won't we? Flora Temple will take a back seat when I get you on the turf, and I reckon old Dexter will just lay down and die when they tell him about you?" With this he began to rub her coat energetically with a brush.

"You're so *cussed* ugly," he began again, "that nobody will ever buy you until you *do* something grand. You'd look well enough if you didn't have yellow legs, and that frost-colored hair! I think I'll dye you when I get you up North—oh, yes, you needn't look 'round, that's where I'm going to take you—ride you all the way, too, maybe, so look around this stable all you can to-day, because before sun-up to-morrow you'll be leaving it forever. I'm sorry, Dewy, but I'm going to use you to make my fortune—sell you, maybe, but I'll have to do it—have to part with you—

but you needn't look mad; I'll get you a good master, and I'll warrant he keeps you like a lady, in a grand stable. Oh, yes, Robert Bonner will buy you soon as he sees you move! Yes, and you'll get into splendid society, Dewy, if you are ugly! Oh, Uncle Phineas don't know *your* gait or he'd never let *you* go. But you're mine! Yes, mine! And we go together, remember that!" So saying he threw the brush into a receptacle in the stone wall of the stable and left the mare with an affectionate "pat."

To Robbie, Dewy Iris was a faithful and obedient subject. To all others she was a willful and ungrateful vixen. She had not, with the exception of her young master, a single friend on the place. Even Phœbe, whose flower-like nature loved nearly every animal on the farm, had for Dewy Iris an indifferent, and lately, a rapidly waning, affection. No one save Robbie could with any certainty ride or drive her. True, like a petted, willful girl with her first beau, she would gracefully and gayly start on a journey, but ere it was half-completed, appear to pout, deliberately and perversely stop; and, though her burden be even the lovely Phœbe, proceed in the most unconventional and ungracious manner to divest herself of it. She employed two methods, either of which was always successful, to accomplish this. One was to sit down on her haunches in the middle of the road, and patiently wait till the rider dismounted. The other was to lie down and roll over. It was noticed she always adopted the former with her lady patrons, and the latter method with her male ones. For this nice discrimination, Phœbe once or twice felt grateful.

However, during the past year, this willful and degenerate animal had so banished all confidence in everybody that Robbie was now her only rider and only defender. She was not always faithful to him, and several times had resented his efforts to have her trot more than two miles at a time on a country road. But she never took dust, or gravel, and would trot ten miles rather than allow any one to pass her. She was the trotting wonder of all the country, but her eccentricities were too well known to make her desired by anybody in that neighborhood.

In a country, once famous for fast horses, a piece of horseflesh possessing the moving qualities of Dewy Iris still excited much admiration. A Kentuckian would have worshiped her the moment he saw her go. Robbie was proud of her. To him she was the surest and swiftest thing he had ever seen. Secretly he had already conceived the plan of taking her to New York, showing her speed to some rich man, and selling her for a fabulous sum. In his confidence he would have staked Dewy Iris against the world. This done, he proposed to get an education, return to Virginia and— marry Phœbe Strong.

With these glowing reflections he proceeded to the carriage house, where the harness and saddles were also kept. He had entered, and, taking down his own saddle and bridle, presents from Phœbe, seated himself on a rude bench near the entrance. He was completely absorbed in examining an apparently weak spot in the surcingle, when he felt upon his shoulder a gentle hand, and looking up, beheld Phœbe gazing tenderly into his face.

CHAPTER XVIII.

PHŒBE'S expression, always sweet, was particularly so just now, and in it was a longing look that made it then not only especially pretty, but wonderfully sympathetic.

"Robbie," she said, and her voice betrayed a trifle unsteadiness, "is thee really going to leave us?"

"Why, sure," somewhat hastily.

"Not to-morrow?"

"To-morrow."

"Robbie, do not go to-morrow! Do not go for another year. Wait another year!"

"Why, Phœbe!" said Robbie, "I—I thought thee would be glad—that is, pleased to see me make a start to—to be somebody. Thee knows, Phœbe, I am bound to have an education, and thee knows I must do something for myself."

"Yes," repressing something in her throat; "yes, of course, but I am thinking of father. Father loves thee; he already leans on thee. I know his heart and his hopes. In another year he will make thee master here, and share with thee the profits of the place."

"Will he do that?" asked Robbie, his heart swelling till his ribs and chest expanded.

"I am sure he will!"

This came very near shattering Robbie's dream of conquest; but recovering himself, and satisfied that his heart had resumed its normal condition, he continued:

"Phœbe, thy father, thy mother and thyself have always discouraged this project of mine, when the time for its execution approached, and heretofore I have listened and yielded.   Now, I will neither listen nor yield.   I will no longer be either the object of pity or the subject of charity.   Your kindness I can never return; your goodness I can never forget, but if I suffer it longer to be exercised, it will kill my ambitions and thwart my purpose.   Fully have I resolved that my life must change.   My mind, Phœbe, is made up.   I am going to school, to college, if I have to scrub floors and sweep dormitories; and then, I am going to study law. I am tired of this listless life; I am tired of being a country clodhopper; I am tired, Phœbe, of being a drab-dressed Quaker.   It's a good thing the Creator of the universe wasn't a Quaker.   All the song birds would have been owls, and all the flowers the color of thy mother's First Day bonnet."

"Why, Robbie!" said Phœbe, completely taken back at the boy's manner and vehemence.

"Of course, the Quakers are all right, Phœbe, and Uncle Phineas and Aunt Rachel will wear wings some day as big and white as the sails of a ship.   But I tell thee, a religion that has neither paintings nor music, singing nor preaching, has about as much chance to last as an Easter bonnet without a feather or flower has for a wearer."

"Robbie, how thee talks!" smiling in spite of herself.

"Yes, I'm talking now, but some day thee'll hear me talk better."

"Thee talks well, I am sure; but I hope thy voice will never be raised against the Quakers."

"It never will, nor against any other sect. Religion, Phœbe, as thee knows, is no part of my life, and will never be any part of my business."

"I think it is a great part of thy life, and thee will never depart from real religion."

"Well, Phœbe, let us not talk about it. Don't try to dissuade me from going, for I am determined. When I return, I will be independent, educated, rich, a gentleman."

"Thee is a gentleman."

"In the rough perhaps, but I'll be in the smooth when I come back."

Phœbe removed her hand from his shoulder and took a parcel from under her apron; it was a small parcel, wrapped in paper. She unwrapped it and displayed a roll of bank bills larger than Robbie had ever seen before.

"Phœbe!" jumping to his feet, "what is thee going to do now?"

"Thee is quite sure thee is going away to-morrow?" She was very firm and womanly now.

"Why, yes."

"Thee is quite sure thee wants to go to school—quite sure thee will go?"

"Yes!"

"THEE HATH NO MONEY—TAKE THIS."

"Thee has no money; no place to go; take this," and she handed him the package.

The generosity of the act and the delicacy of its execution touched him to the heart. He leaned his flushed face against the cold tire of the wagon wheel, and the tears trickled through his fingers like rain, coursing down the tire till they dropped to the floor. She saw his emotion; her own feelings were fast overcoming her. As he did not reach for the money, she laid it on the mud dasher of the vehicle against which he leaned, and gathering her drab dress about her, literally flew from his presence.

CHAPTER XIX.

WHEN Robbie looked up and brushed away the tears
he was alone. Before him reposed the pile of money!

"When I take it," thought the lad, "I hope my
hands will turn to ashes!"

This money, which was something more than one
thousand dollars, represented the careful savings of
Phœbe's life. It was the sole worldly thing she could
unqualifiedly call her own. It had been more than
twenty years reaching its present proportions. It
represented the proceeds of sales from pet pigs, fat
steers, horses, colts, calves, lambs, sheep, strutting
turkeys, and crowing chanticleers, given to her from
time to time by her generous, indulgent father.

Once or twice a year, ever since she was a little girl,
Phineas would take her to the field, the pig sty, the
sheep fold, or the stables, and present her with some
member of his various flocks. Sometimes it was a
lamb, innocent and bleating, who would soon become
her special care, eat from her hand, and follow her
about till at last it met the fate of its fellows, and was led
to the shambles. Sometimes it was a cute and blink-
ing little porker, with a tail like a gimlet and an appe-
tite like an elephant, who was allowed to root, squeal
or grunt his way into her affections, and then at last,

his gratitude stunted by accumulated adipose and his eyes closed in sluggish, swinish indifference, he, too, would be allowed to join the "choir invisible," and make room for another love, another object, for the concern and care of solicitous Phœbe. Several times he had given her colts to raise, Jersey heifers, calves, and once, after Robbie came, a pair of steers to break, which she, with the boy's assistance, trained into two dignified and obedient oxen, and sold them to "Cat" Doggett for seventy-five dollars, dividing the money with Robbie. Some of her horses brought good prices in Washington, and one which she had broken herself was shipped there and, she had been told, purchased by President Grant.

Of late years the income from the butter and poultry, such as was not exchanged at the stores for sugar, salt, muslin, gingham and shoes, was equally divided between her and her mother.

In this way Phineas Strong not only contrived to supply the women of the house with ample pocket money, but stimulated their interest and encouraged their thrift and independence by supplying the means whereby they could earn it. Thus examples of his generosity were constantly before them, while they, in the exercise of their innocent rivalry for his praise, were always in the enjoyment of that rare felicity which comes from the successful achievement of individual efforts.

Robbie, therefore knew better than anybody else the sweet ardor which had helped accumulate this money.

Every bank bill before him had a history, and in Phœbe's mind it must always be associated with the thought of a pet horse, a gentle lamb, or a sad-eyed, warm breathing Jersey heifer.

Why, around that pile of money hung a halo of recollections as sweet and tender as the memories of a buried love. Every bill had been wet by Phœbe's tears, and Robbie knew it. To him those notes were as sacred as are the dead, scentless posies pressed into the leaves of some yellow-paged book by the hand of—well, say the hand of a sainted mother.

"Well," he said, trying to repress the coming tears, "I couldn't take money from a woman; anyhow, I couldn't take her money; and that money," eyeing the parcel, "well, I couldn't take that if I was starving! Why, Robert Porter," talking to himself, "if you take that money, I'll kill you, yes, kill you dead and throw your body into the river for the fish to feed on!"

Delivering himself thus rather vehemently, he took a pencil, and wrote on a portion of the paper which partly concealed the bank notes:

"DEAREST FRIEND PHŒBE (how he wished he dared leave out the 'friend'): I couldn't take thy money. Indeed, I could not. I have Dewy Iris, and nearly three hundred dollars, counting the two hundred Uncle Phineas gave me this morning. Don't, please, don't, offer me the money again. I couldn't even borrow it of thee. It would always make me feel mean to take it—besides uncle would lend me money if I wanted it.

I want to earn my own money, and not be a beggar. But, Phœbe, some day, thee will know how I thank thee.   ROBBIE."

This was the first letter Robbie had ever written in his life, and he read it several times before he concluded to fold it and the money together, and dispatch them by the hand of a servant to the presence of their noble and unselfish owner. To deliver them himself was a task, just now, he dare not trust himself to attempt. He had completed the folding and tying of the package, when Betty, the cook, evidently just from an excursion in search of fresh eggs, holding her apron up and folded about her two hands, appeared, passing the door of the carriage house.

"Oh, Betty!" called Robbie, "do me a favor?"

"Dat will I," says Betty. "What you want me to do, Mas'r Bob?"

"Here's a parcel Phœbe dropped a moment ago. Carry it to her right away."

"Suah, is dat all?"

"That is all, Betty, and here is something for your trouble."

With that he put the package in her apron, and passed before her eyes a brand-new dollar bill.

"What's dat for, Mas'r Bob?"

"For your trouble."

"Fo' my trouble?"

"Yes!"

"I hain't got no trouble, Mas'r Bob."

"No?"

"Neber had no trouble sence Mas'r Strong ben on de place."

"Oh, I mean this," passing the dollar bill close to her eyes, "is to pay you for doing my errand!"

"Is dat a dolla'?"

"Yes."

"It ain't no real dolla'?"

"Yes, real and good!"

"Look here, Mas'r Bob, is you goin' to gib me a dolla' for takin' dat passel ter Miss Phœbe?"

"Certainly!"

"Keep yo' dolla', boy! you'se puttin' on dis mornin'. Has Mas'r Strong done gib yo' de place?"

"Betty, you have always been kind to me. I am going to leave early to-morrow morning, and wanted— felt like giving you a trifle."

The clasped hands under the apron parted, up went the arms, and away went the package, and smash on the ground went the eggs.

"Goin' ter do what, chile?"

"Going to leave."

"To leave dis here place?"

"Yes."

"Look here, Mas'r Bob, what's gittin' into dis place? Missus hain't spoke to me fer two hours. Yer uncle done tole me jes now to quit singin', and Miss Phœbe was outen de back po'ch all de mornin' cryin';—I seed her my o'nself; and now, you offers me a dolla', and den says yo' is goin' away. No, 'tain't true! You won't go, Mas'r Bob, dey won't let yer. W'en yo' goes 'way from here I reckon de mour'in' badges will be blacker dan any nigger's face in dese parts. Dey won't hang up no drab crape fo' yo', Mas'r Bob. Allus kno'd yo' was fuller'n dem jokes and tricks, but yer can't play no game wid dis chicken. I'll take yer passel, an' gib it to de lady; but yer dis keep de dolla' bill. I'se goin' to hab custa'd pie fer dinner, ef these eggs ain't all busted." She stooped down and gathered all she could, and the "passel" into her apron. "Nex' time, Mas'r Bob, you makes me break a dozen eggs wif yo' fool 'nouncements, I'll break yo' hed!"

She waddled toward the house, where in a few moments she placed the "passel" in Phœbe's hands, and nearly lost her breath when Phœbe, to her inquiries, assured her that she believed Robbie would leave them on the morrow.

CHAPTER XX.

MUCH was the consternation among the colored people when it was generally known that Robbie was going away. They all loved him. During the day most of them had been to him and begged him not to go.

If then, this character, my hero, could awaken in the dusky servants sentiments of the sincerest friendship these simple people could ever know, what tender ties must have grown between him and the Strongs, to whom his frankness, his generosity, his memory and his genial, sunny temper had for many years among themselves been the chief charm of their lives, and the most frequent subject of their conversation?

It was "Robbie" here, and "Robbie" there, and "Robbie" this, and "Robbie" that, and fondness daily expended itself in petty praises and tender endearments. Why he ever wanted to leave was a mystery to all. In after years Robbie learned there was no correct solution for the query.

To Phœbe, more than all others, the prospect of his going brought the most disquiet, the most anguish. All day she had racked her brain for some plan to prevent it. At dinner she ate nothing. In the evening when the sun had disappeared behind the western treetops in a bank of somber clouds, her eyes were red and her head was throbbing. Her feelings when Betty returned the money, and when she had read the note, were wrought to the highest pitch. She indulged in an uncontrollable fit of weeping, which lasted more than an hour.

For years she had come to regard Robbie as her own. The possibility of his actually going away never was fully realized; indeed, until now it had never been considered. She did not see, could not bring herself to understand, why he must go. The terrible tugging pains about her heart told her too plainly she could never witness his departure without complete collapse. His going was a serious thing to poor Phœbe. Her affection had become a love, a passion that occupied her whole being. For years she had dreamed, planned, and thought only of Robbie. That he would some day come to her and lay his heart at her feet, she firmly believed. That he did not now declare himself she attributed to his pride, his poverty, his youth. His noble nature, she felt sure, alone restrained the declaration of that passion which she was confident burned in his bosom as brightly and as constantly as in her own.

But to part from him, to see him go away; to think of him alone in the world, battling for life, too proud to ask or accept assistance; to think of the passing days, the long nights, the weeks, months, perhaps years before she might again see his face; for she knew he would return only when he had accomplished his purpose. And she, who had plenty, could not even help

him; she of all the world; she, who would have followed him barefooted, if necessary, through the universe.   Then the dread that he might never return, that
some other face might charm him more than her own,
the dread that when he did come she would be too old,
too plain.

"Oh, surely," she thought, "before he goes he will
tell me.   Surely he will ask me to wait for him.
Surely he will say something; surely he must see, must
know, how dearly I love him!   Oh, I can't let him go,
I know I can't!   I might as well die!   Something will
happen to make him understand.   Oh, if I dared, if he
wouldn't despise me, I would throw my arms about
him and tell him!   But no, he would hate me then.   I
know him.   He is going away to win me.   He has said
it almost.   I suppose it is to be.   But it is hard, so
hard to bear!"   And it was.

The poor girl spent most of the day in tears, and by
the time night set in was really sick of grief.   She kept
her room until quite late, and just before the family
was about to retire, appeared in the sitting room, where
her mother, her father and Robbie were making prelim-
inary movements for bed.

Now, reader, Phœbe had a becoming amount of
dignity, and entirely too much pride to betray her emotions in public, or confide to even her parents so dear a
secret as her love for Robbie Porter.   It was her own,
and she did not propose to impart its knowledge to
others.   Therefore, despite the tears and agitation of
the day, she presented a most charming appearance.

She informed the company that she was better, and told Robbie she would wait till morning to bid him "farewell."

"Please wake me as thee comes down," she said, "for I want to wish thee fair winds and a prosperous voyage." Behind a smiling face she concealed the day's ravages an aching heart had left there.

"I am going to Fredericksburg, and from there by boat to Baltimore, and from there by boat to New York," said Robbie; "so I will be up with the lark."

"Will thee wear thy good clothes?" asked Aunt Rachel.

"Yes," said Robbie, "and I wish thee would lay them out for me to-night!"

"Very well; I will put them right across the foot of thy bed, and thee will see them as soon as thee opens thy eyes. Farewell, Robert," she said; "thee must write to us. Be as good in the world as thou hast been here and thee need never be ashamed of thy conduct. Fare thee well."

This dear, motherly woman, now nearly threescore and ten, turned from him the sweetest, most placid face he ever saw, and left the room, whence all soon after dispersed, Phœbe to her apartment, and Robbie to his attic; where, alone, he proceeded to complete his preparations for the morning.

His wardrobe was not extensive. He had intended to pack it in his father's old knapsack and take it with him. He therefore proceeded to hunt for this relic, but upon discovering it and bringing it to the light, decided that it was too much worn, and the brass plate, with the U. S. engraved thereon, might be misleading. He, therefore, without even disturbing or looking at the papers or letters within, kicked it into a corner, placed an open-faced silver watch, a present from Aunt Rachel, under his pillow, disrobed, pinched the light from his candle with his thumb and forefinger, and jumped into bed.

Every night for seven years he had slept in that bed, in that room. It was a large, plainly furnished apartment, partitioned off at the north side of the attic, and lighted and ventilated by means of a large square window, composed of Colonial panes of glass, of almost innumerable quantity. This window was fastened to the window frame by means of hinges, and opened and shut with a lateral motion. When closed it could be firmly secured by means of a hickory button or knob which occupied a middle position on that side of the window frame opposite the hinges. This button was held in place by a screw in its center, so adjusted that usually a slight touch of the finger and thumb were sufficient to move it up or down, so that when the window was closed the horizontal position of the button was sufficient to keep it so.

The walls and ceiling were plastered and "white-washed." The floor was white oak, and was devoid of carpet, rug or matting. A bedstead, painted red, on which was a huge featherbed, supported by ropes beneath; a red chest in a corner, an old-fashioned red chair, with a white seat made of twisted corn husks, and an old mahogany-veneered work-stand, with sides raised above the topmost shelf, and rolled at the ends into a scroll like a Queen Elizabeth collar, completed the furnishings of the room. It was clean, plain, severe, yet comfortable, and yet, reader, you will agree with me that it was not wholly attractive. With the exception of Phœbe's, and two spare rooms, few of the apartments in the house were but little more elaborate.

Upon the floor in Phœbe's room there was a rag carpet, which she and her mother had made, and which was woven by the colored help on the farm.

Robbie, to whom usually sleep came at his bidding, found in a little while that his sensations and his thoughts were repelling all semblance to drowsiness. He would close his eyes, but he could not lose consciousness. Try as he would, he could not banish Phœbe's face from his mind. It seemed to haunt him. Her expression in the carriage house, the wistful, longing look appealed to him, and seemed to cry out, to ask for something; to beseech, and yet conceal the very request it would make. The information conveyed to him by Betty that she had seen Phœbe weeping also made a deep impression. He did not flatter himself, however, that she wept over the prospect of his departure.

"Of course," reasoned he mentally, "she might be crying about my going, but then she'd cry if she sold a pet pig or lost a bird. I'm a fool to think of her in the way I do. She wouldn't notice me—she will some day. She won't marry. There is no one here good enough for her, and she never goes from home. Besides, when I get to New York I'll write it to her; tell her I love her, and ask her to wait for me. Then, if she laughs I can't hear her; you can't write a laugh, and she's too good to hurt my feelings in a letter. I'll come and see her if she says yes; if she doesn't—well—I'll go to the devil, I guess."

With visions of Phœbe before him, chasing away by her words-to-be the prospects of his going to the devil, he at last fell asleep.

CHAPTER XXI.

IT chanced that on this particular night the window button, whose duty it was to hold the window of Robbie's room in its place when closed, had carelessly been left in a perpendicular position.

Sleep, which had been kind to our hero, was cruel to Phœbe, and left her entirely to the solitude of reflection. Therefore, when the wind arose among the swaying trees, she heard it; and when the rain beat against her window pane, she hoped it would continue in torrents so Robbie could not go on the morrow. At this very moment an increased blast of the storm without rattled all the windows of the house, and she was quite sure had blown one open. In the intervals of stillness that followed, she listened intently in the darkness; yes, she was sure Robbie's window had blown open, and was swinging to and fro, knocking against the wall, causing a clanging and a banging noise that must sooner or later shatter every pane in the sash. She could occasionally hear sheets of rain sweep in and fall upon the floor and bed.

"Robbie must be asleep," she thought, "or surely he would close the window. He will get his death of cold!"

Here all of her natural sympathies began to disturb

her little heart; and, all unconscious of the semi-hidden charms the dim light of a tallow candle revealed, she noiselessly proceeded to ascend the stairs leading to Robbie's room.

At the threshold of his door she paused, and for an instant hesitated to enter. Some thought, perhaps the impropriety of the situation, may have arrested her, but only for a moment. Why should it? Her motive was noble, and conscious of her purity and innocence, all scruples vanished.

How many times, how many hundred times, had she stood by that boy's bedside, and watched that sweet smile, which always played round his mouth, sleeping or waking. How often had she entered that very room and done what she came to do now—close his window against the storms that threatened his health. How often had she tucked the coverlet about his form, kissed his smooth, white forehead, and, undiscovered, escaped to the secrecy of her own room.

She would close his window once more. She would tuck the coverlet around him, and—yes, once more kiss him. Her mind, full of goodness, and her heart full of love, the candle elevated before her face, her lovely charms of breast and neck struggling here and there in red and white patches between the ruffles and frills of her gown; her feet bare, her long, rich black hair streaming behind her, she entered the presence of the sleeper, and tiptoed her way, passing the footboard of the bed, to the open and refractory window. Quickly, noiselessly and securely, she thought, she fastened it by

SHE ENTERED THE ROOM OF THE SLEEPER.

means of the hickory button. Turning, she retraced
her steps, crossed to the other side of the bed, and stood
looking into Robbie's face. A puddle of rain water
was spreading itself into a little lake under the bed, and
it now reached her bare feet. The coverlet at the side
nearest the window and near the footboard was sop-
ping wet, and there lay our hero, his arms thrown up
and resting on the pillow back of his head.

His lips, pouting into a sweet expression, at this
instant parted, and a smile played along their edges from
every curve and corner. His shirt collar rolled back,
and opened below the band; the coverlet thrown back, his
neck and chest were completely exposed to the inclement
storm. Delicately she leaned over (he was sleeping
soundly now) and nimbly fastened his shirt collar so as to
conceal his exposed chest. She then carefully drew up
the coverlet. To do this completely and properly, it
was necessary to relinquish her hold on the candle.
She therefore placed it on the coverlet on that side nearest the window, and in a spot somewhat smooth and flat,
and not occupied by any part of the sleeper. This
done, she leaned over those smiling lips and kissed
them.

At that very moment, I think, Robbie must have
been dreaming, and the dream must have been of the
fair girl who was pressing her face to his. It must
have been a palpable dream, for his lips parted, and
the word "Phœbe" issued from them with a sweet but
startling distinctness.

At the same moment, involuntarily yielding no

doubt to the impulse of the delicious dream which was then floating before his slumbering vision, his arms raised from the pillow, encircled the head and neck of the half-reclining Phœbe, and drawing her down upon his breast, held her in a vise-like embrace.

Poor Phœbe! The world was sliding from under her feet. In the vigor of that strong grasp her own strength left her, and her whole body became like warm wax.

She thought him awake. He was in fact asleep; and yet he hugged her all the tighter. She tried to extricate herself, and in her efforts overturned the candle stick. Out went the light, and its lead stick and platter fell from the bed to the floor. With a muffled sound they rolled to the further end of the room.

"Robbie! Robbie! Robbie!" whispered Phœbe, "please let me go; wake up, Robbie!" and Robbie awoke to a realization of his dream. Phœbe Strong was fast in his arms, and her warm, sweet breath was blowing its delicious fragrance into his face. He sat bolt upright, felt with his fingers her face and hair, felt the warm, velvety softness of that cheek which always bloomed like a rose. At last, dimly comprehending the cause of the sudden sensation of happiness which was stealing over his frame, he exclaimed:

"Phœbe! Is it thee, Phœbe?"

"Yes, Robbie, the wind blew open thy window. I came to shut it, and to pull the coverlet over thee. Thee caught hold of me."

"Oh, Phœbe, did I do that?" he said, falling back

on the pillow, and holding her hand in one of his; "did I really do that? Oh, Phœbe! Forgive me, will thee? I didn't know what I was doing; forgive me, Phœbe."

"I forgive thee, Robert. Now let me go!"

Involuntarily—it seemed that it must have been so—his own courage never could have done it—his arms reached out and enfolded that divine creature, drew her head down beside his own, and in a voice, the dryness of his lips and mouth reduced to the faintest whisper, said, "Oh, Phœbe, how I love thee! Wait for me, Phœbe, till I come back. I have loved thee ever since I saw thee; I will love thee till I die!"

Alas, for Phœbe! She knew it all now. The something had happened. Robbie loved her. She was too happy to even speak. Her limbs fell a-trembling, her muscles relaxed, and down into the pools of water that covered the floor she slipped to her knees. Around her waist, resting on her hips went Robbie's strong right arm; with it he pressed her form against the side of the bed, and her head fell over on his bosom.

"Oh, Robbie! Does thee mean it?"

"Does thee love me?"

"Couldn't thee see that I loved thee?"

"No, I couldn't; but does thee? Will thee, Phœbe, marry me when I come back?"

"Yes, Robbie, I love thee! I will marry thee when thee comes back! I will marry thee to-morrow; I will never marry anybody but thee!"

"Phœbe, Phœbe!" he exclaimed, "I never dared

think it. I don't deserve it, but thee wouldn't say it if thee didn't mean it, would thee, Phœbe?"

"No," said Phœbe, and immediately fell a-trembling as though shaken with an ague.

Passively she still knelt. All of the sweet, pure, maidenly impulses of her nature crowded into her mind, and urged her to fly from the scene, but the mystic spell, the indefinable sweetness of the whole situation, the joy in her heart, the knowledge that her love was returned, the sudden realization that he was hers, hers for all time, drove away her impulses to flight. The night concealed her blushes; and her agitation, her happiness, silenced the rising protest of her tongue, and chained her to the spot.

In the depth of her great love, and in the purity of her heart, as well as its longings, she thought no wrong, and saw no harm. In the mighty scope of that passion which for five years had been her thought by day and her dream by night, she found justification and stilled the voice of conscience. No matter now what would happen, or what could happen, Robbie was hers! Their troth was plighted, eternal vows were exchanged, and these two, whom the Creator no doubt long ago designed each for the other, in that dark, wet room of that old attic, alone, while the storm lashed and fumed without, revealed their mutual love, and if either could have beheld the face of the other, it would have been to read life's meaning in each other's eyes.

CHAPTER XXII.

Now, of course, my lady readers are breaking out into exclamations of surprise at the weakness of Phœbe.

No doubt her conduct will be condemned, and her name deprecated; but, fair reader, she has a champion in the author. By Heaven, miss or madam, if you please, she was not weak. It takes a lasting love to risk what Phœbe risked. It takes a world of confidence in the object of your affection to do what Phœbe did. It takes a strong character to brave a censorious community who knows a woman's first misstep. It takes a brave heart in a mother to face and go through the world with the offspring of an illicit love. It takes a noble woman to see in the living evidence of her shame the personification of her trust.

Perhaps Phœbe did not think of these things, perhaps did not carefully consider them; but Phœbe was now a woman, mentally and physically matured. She knew all these things, she considered them all, and, weighing the praise and censure of the world with the joy of this revealed love, resolved to enjoy the one, and if necessary, endure the other.

And what then? Nothing, reader! There is nothing beyond the flowered fruition of a first love.

"Whether there be prophecies, they shall fail:

whether there be tongues they shall cease, and whether there be knowledge it shall vanish away," but the remembrance of a first love, reciprocated, fulfilled, will linger on and on, and in the halls of memory be carried even beyond the portals of time.

And if, in the gloomy cave of the mountain fastness, Æneas and Dido were married, then Robbie and Phœbe were married. It needed no mumbling preacher, no smirking attendants, no strains of music, no fulsome praises to add sacredness to a union like theirs. The law would have been powerless to have welded these hearts closer, or mingled and blended so completely the lives, the hopes, the purposes and plans of two people more perfectly. True, they were married as nature marries; they were married as the birds marry; they were married as marry the lilies of the ponds and the flowers of the field; and, unknowingly, each of them, their two natures teeming with passion and overflowing with affection, yielded, bowed submissive to a primeval law, older even than the laws of God and higher than the laws of man.

Phœbe was still good, still pure, still innocent, still beautiful, and better than all, she was happy.

CHAPTER XXIII.

AND, reader, whether there be nights of pain, or nights of pleasure; whether there be nights of grief, or nights of sorrow, the morning will come just as sure as time will be measured. To some the day brings the harp of love, and to others the scourge of hate. On its breath is sometimes borne the fragrance of happiness, and sometimes the stench of misery.

To Robbie the morning came and with it a realization of all that had taken place. And now, more than ever, he determined that he must leave. Now, it would never do to stay. He must go, do something quick; and, with fame sounding in his ears, fortune in his hands, return and claim before the world his beautiful bride. She had promised to wait. She had said the words. He believed her implicitly. He would have strangled the suggestion of a doubt. "No! No! there is no doubt in that bosom; no wavering in that heart!"

Quickly dressing in his best suit, a brown-colored cassimere, consisting of roundabout coat, a vest, and a pair of trousers, all made by Phœbe, he approached that side of the bed on which she lay, and stood for a moment affectionately gazing into that perfect, upturned, happy face.

She slept soundly, peacefully. It was barely day,

not six o'clock. Not a soul was stirring. "I will not wake her! Let her sleep. It is better so!" he said.

He leaned over the prostrate form, and fearing lest she wake, to press his lips to hers, gathered in one hand the strands of silken hair that lay loosely upon the pillow, and winding them around his neck for a minute, kissed them again and again, replaced them, picked up his top boots and rapidly quitted the room.

An uncontrollable desire seized him to get away. He was stifling till he reached the open air. Waiting for neither toilet nor breakfast, seeing nobody, he hastened to the barn, threw the saddle on Dewy Iris, felt to see if his money was in his vest pocket, mounted, and urged the creature hastily forward.

The tears were coursing down his cheeks as he passed rapidly along that very road that first led him to this sweet retreat; this dear home. The rain, instead of abating, increased in volume, and the wind in fury.

From the overhanging trees as he rode along, great flakes and sheets of water dropped over him, and soon he was wet to the skin. He had no top coat, and had not proceeded more than a few miles when a sense of chilliness stole over his frame. His emotions were the saddest he had ever known. He condemned himself as a fool with nearly every stride of his horse.

Once, reader, yes, once, he turned the animal about, and galloped back to within sight of the "whitewashed gate," and the old, white-painted house. But his pride would not suffer him to enter. Again he headed

Dewy Iris toward Fredericksburg. This time he dried his eyes, swore inwardly he would never shed another tear as long as he lived, and, despite the mud, the rain, the pools, the wet leaves, and the slashing branches, his slouch hat almost concealing his face, fairly flew toward his destination, where he arrived about nine o'clock, and learned that the boat, due to sail at ten, would not, on account of some repairs, leave till six o'clock in the evening.

And what a sight horse and rider were as they appeared that day before the doors of a livery stable and sought admission.

Robbie was wet, bespattered, bedraggled, cold, hungry, and in no very pleasant mood. Dewy Iris was coated with red and white clay, mixed with big patches of black mud. Her sides were working in and out like a bellows, and diffusing clouds of steam like a resting locomotive.

"Specs you had quite a chase," remarked a colored hostler, appearing in response to Robbie's halloo, and keeping his eyes on Dewy Iris.

"Feed her as soon as she stops steaming," said Robbie "then groom her till you get every speck of mud and every bit of dirt out of her hair. Be careful, too, or she'll kick your brains out. I'll be after her before five o'clock."

"Peart animal?" queried the negro.

"Rather!" said Robbie. "If you think you've got anything in this barn that can give her dust, just say to your friends that I've got three hundred dollars right here," tapping that side of the vest where reposed his money.

"Dere's a gem'man stoppin' cross there to the tav'rn, got two hosses inside says got records of 2 :22. Rec'on he'll chew up dat money, ef you wants to lose it. He's right ober dere now, ef yer wants ter see him."

Here he led Dewy Iris through the open door.

"All right," answered Robbie cheerily, "if there's any game in him, I'll get his money." With that he strode across the street, and entered the main room or office of the tavern.

The little town of Fredericksburg, between the base of a ridge of hills on the right, and the Rappahannock River on its left, nestled in its inanimate repose and undisturbed tranquillity. Tumbling dissolution made the walls of the former business blocks and houses, seared with shells, and blackened by fire, repelling and cheerless. War, awful war, had not wholly withdrawn its baneful shadow. The former homes of elegance and wealth were paintless, fenceless, and falling with decay. Three or four thousand people found homes within its boundaries, the majority of whom were members of that helpless race the misdirected efforts of war had thrown upon a hopeless, impoverished community. They stood on the corners, loafed in the stores, and shambled along the streets, ragged, shoeless, aimless.

In the town there was then neither enterprise nor thrift. Even the marble shaft hauled there years ago to commemorate the resting place of the mother of

Washington, lay at the base of the pedestal, sinking into the soft earth. The liveliest places in the town were the National and Confederate cemeteries.

The hotel, or public house, Robbie entered, was a low, two-story brick building, standing somewhat back of the mud road that led before it to the boat landing. It was conducted by a woman whose husband had perished on the battlefield in front of Marye's Heights. A horde of half-clothed negro men and women made up the "help" of the house.

At one end of the room, toward the east, was a huge fireplace, and in it was a pile of pine knots and oak logs, all ablaze. Three men, with their chairs tipped back, sat before the fire. Behind the chimney, and in the corner, a half-grown, half-naked negro boy slept in unconscious, undisturbed serenity. Shiftlessness marked the whole interior. The blazing pine was the only cheerful thing in sight, and toward it, extending his hands, Robbie moved. Each gentleman "hitched" his chair a little as he drew near, and one of them, spare, gray-haired, nice looking, dressed in black, with spotless linen and carefully polished shoes, his wrists adorned with cuffs, and his hair brushed and carefully curled into a shiny roll about his neck, looked up and said: "Wet day, sir!"

This was an observation both trite and true, but the manner of its delivery indicated the deliverer a man of refinement and social instincts. His was a clear-cut but kind face. His fastidious dress and appearance indicated him not only a man of wealth, but of experience, taste and education. How true it is that unconsciously we betray our birth and breeding, and this man, to Robbie's limited knowledge of the world, conveyed the idea that both were good. To him, therefore, in spite of his uncomfortable feelings, he addressed a pleasant but modest reply:

"Yes, sir, wet riding and muddy traveling."

"Ride far?"

"Fifteen miles." He had in fact ridden nineteen.

"Through this rain?"

"Yes, sir."

"You and your horse, sir, must be tired; heavy going, wasn't it?"

"Most of the way was very heavy!"

"And your horse, sir?" asked the gentleman, craning his neck toward the window.

"In the barn!" indicating by a motion of the head the direction.

"That's right! I like to see a man care for his horse first!" This was said very approvingly.

"Yes," replied Robbie, "the horse is faithful and fearless. I love my horse!"

If Robbie had known his auditor all his life and known his foibles and his weaknesses, and had deliberately planned some remark to flatter and to please him and to win his heart, he could have said nothing more calculated to effect this than what he had just uttered.

Quick, very quick for one of his years, the old man sprang to his feet, and making a step or two, seized Robbie's hand.

"Pardon me, sir, but your sentiment marks you a youth of sense and mercy.   Believe me, I am pleased to meet you.   Accept my friendship, sir, and honor me with yours in return.   Permit me, sir, to offer you my card!"   He handed Robbie a rectangular piece of cardboard on which, printed in black letters, was:

"S. P. BOWERS,
                    "Lancaster, Pa.
"Judge Court Common Pleas."

To be noticed and commended by a judge; to have his friendship and esteem, you may be sure, were honors already Robbie never dreamed to enjoy.   His surprise, his pleasure for the moment, restrained his reply.   His ready wit, however, came to his aid, and bowing, he spake:

"You do me great honor, sir, by your condescension. Your friendship I should prize.   I sir, am poor, obscure, unlearned.   In the language of Marc Antony, 'I have neither wit, wisdom, eloquence, nor words.' My friendship would be useless to a man like you.   I have no card; I never saw one before.   My name is Robert Porter.   I am starting to-day into the world to get a name like yours, to seek a home and win a fortune.   If all my hopes become as damp as my clothes, I make no doubt that at the end of my journey I will present a sorry plight!"

This little speech pleased Judge Bowers, and so attracted the attention of the other gentlemen that they could not forbear looking with considerable interest, not wholly devoid of admiration.

"Young man," said the judge, "if I read your face rightly, you will be much wetter than you are to-day when you present a sorry plight. Where do you go?"

"To Baltimore by boat; thence to New York by boat."

"How fortunate. I leave by boat for Baltimore this evening. Going to take home a couple of brood mares. Got two high steppers in the barn. Little old, but fast, wonderfully fast. I shall breed them. Got them out here at Orange from a friend of mine, located there from near Lancaster. Glad to know we will be fellow-passengers. Engaged your stateroom?"

"No, sir," said Robbie. "It costs a dollar extra."

"So it does; so it does. Well, share mine! Plenty room for two, and I'd be glad of your company!"

"Thank you, sir. Thank you, but——"

"No but about it. Consider yourself my guest. Stopping here? Well, dine with me to-day. Here, you boy!" pushing the chair leg of the sleeping negro with his foot. "Here, you slave of Morpheus, go tell your mistress that Mr. Porter dines with me, and if that boat doesn't go at six, sups with me also. Tell her to put his reckoning with mine. Allow me," turning again to Robbie, "sir, to consider myself fortunate at the prospect of so agreeable a companion. After dinner I'll show you my mares!"

CHAPTER XXIV.

IN the company of a man like Judge Bowers, whose conversation possessed the charm of elegant diction, the balance of the morning soon passed, and the midday meal was announced. Intent upon filling up space for two meals with what was originally intended for one, Robbie took no part in the conversation. While it is true, he listened attentively to all that was said, his youth, and perhaps modesty, as well as his hunger, kept him silent. The company, however, talked incessantly. The Tenure of Office Act, the Great Impeachment trial, Reconstruction, President Grant, and, lastly, the character of the late president, Andrew Johnson, and his inhumanity in not preventing the hanging of Mrs. Suratt, charged with being accessory to the murder of President Lincoln.

Here the talk waxed warm, and the judge's plea for mercy for the woman, who he claimed was not legally convicted, was received by the majority with neither grace nor favor. Seeing, therefore, that he was on the unpopular side, he looked across the table appealingly to our hero, and said:

"What say you, Mr. Porter? Give us your views!"

To be addressed as "Mr." Porter, and to be referred to for his opinion, was so flattering to Robbie that he hurriedly swallowed a half-masticated piece of boiled beef, and thus delivered himself:

"Of the justice or injustice of the execution of Mrs. Suratt, I have really never thought. Chivalry will always be on the side of woman; but it may sometimes happen that the laws will be exercised against the sins of human kind, irrespective of sex. Of this, however, I am, from my limited reading and more limited observation, almost ready to conclude, that neither king nor president, in the administration of duties, will ever win unqualified approval. One-half the world will praise what he has done, and the other half denounce what he has left undone. Appropriately I may here observe the language of Chief Justice Storey: 'Perfect justice belongs to one Judgment Seat only, and that which is linked to the Throne of God. Human reason seems powerless to attain it!' "

The entire assembly had listened, spellbound with astonishment. Judge Bowers jumped to his feet, reached across the table, and with undoubted sincerity and unfeigned enthusiasm, said:

"Your hand, sir. Your hand! I applaud your sentiments. I see you are a youth of reading and of reflection. I am proud, sir, to know a man who can quote from Justice Storey! Let us look at the horses."

"There!" exclaimed the judge, entering the stable, and affectionately laying his hand on the rump of a large, spare-fleshed bay mare, "there's grace and speed, sir! There's blood; there's endurance; trotted on the

Strasburg track, three in five, in two twenty-two only a year ago! Oh, she's a goer!"

"Good wind?" said Robbie."

"Perfect, sir! Trot ten miles and never turn a hair! Wonderful, sir! wonderful! Sold her colt last year for a thousand dollars! Got your horse here?"

"There she is, sir!" pointing to Dewy Iris, at the opposite side of the stable, now groomed into passable respectability. Judge Bowers eyed her from nose to tail, from fetlocks to withers.

"Gentle?"

"As a lamb!"

"Three or four years old?"

"Just turned four."

"Remarkable combination of coloring!"

"Yes; little odd."

"Standard?"

"Yes, sir!"

"Registered?"

"No!"

"By performance, then?"

"By performance."

"What track?"

"On the big road!"

"Time?"

"Oh, about two twenty!"

Judge Bowers looked at Robbie seriously for a minute, and seeing he was in dead earnest, said: "Young man, if your mare can trot a mile in two minutes. and twenty seconds, I'll give you five thousand dollars for

her, cash, the moment we can land her in Lancaster!"

Five thousand dollars was really more ready money
than Robbie conceived to be in the possession of one
man at one time. The magnitude almost stunned him.
His friend's tone, and the expression of his face, quickly
assured him, however, that the judge meant it!

"Judge Bowers," he said, "you are a stranger to
me, but I believe you are sincere. I will sell you my
mare. I will undertake to deliver her safely into your
barn in Lancaster, at my own expense, but I propose a
modification of your offer!"

"Well."

"The mare is yours. You pay me in hand two thousand dollars. I will agree to live in the town where
you take her, and drive her daily, and will agree at any
time within a year to drive her one mile on any track
you name, inside of two minutes and eighteen seconds,
or refund the two thousand dollars you advance. You
then, if I succeed, pay me the three thousand dollars."

"That's hardly the proposition."

"Can your mare trot in two twenty-two?"

"Yes," slowly.

"Well, then, I'll put up," and here he produced his
wallet, "three hundred against one hundred dollars
with any one you name, and hitch up now, that I can
beat your mare four seconds, you to be the judge."

The money was here counted, and Robbie had about
nine dollars remaining.

Judge Bowers was convinced that the young man

meant business, and knew exactly what he was talking about; in short, he had already great confidence in Robbie, and frankly and manfully spoke: "I won't bet, but I accept your terms on one condition, that you will live in my house, and take care of the animal!"

"Good schools and colleges there?"

"Best in the world!"

"It's a bargain!"

"It's a bargain," repeated the judge.

"The mare is yours."

"The mare is mine," said the judge. "Come across to the hotel, and I will draw a receipt."

They walked together across the street. Judge Bowers opened his valise, took therefrom a sheet of paper, a small, rectangular book, and going to the desk, wrote on a leaf in the little book a check for two thousand dollars, on the Lancaster National Bank, payable to the order of Robert Porter, Esq., signed his name, and wrote a bill as follows:

"FREDERICKSBURG, Va., Nov. 5, 1869.
"S. P. BOWERS,
"TO ROBERT PORTER, DR.
"To one mare, four-year old, known as Dewy Iris,
  $5,000.
"Rec'd on acct. two thousand dollars."

He handed Robbie the bill, and when it was signed, handed him the check.

Robbie had never seen a check on a bank before in his life, but he made no doubt it was just the same as money.

"Now," said the judge, "perhaps we had better have a little written agreement between us."

"As far as I am concerned," replied Robbie, "I will take your word. I never want to do business with a man whose word is not as sacred as his writing."

"Good!" said the judge. "I trust you, sir!"

"I trust you also, and to show you that I do, take back the check. Keep it for me till the day I complete my part of the contract," Robbie replied, and handed back the check.

This act completed Judge Bowers' estimate of Robert Porter. He saw in him a frank, confiding, yet resolute youth, whose purpose once formed, would, in all human probability, be executed. He already felt that, barring the death of, or accident to, Dewy Iris, he would have to pay that three thousand dollars.

In Judge Bowers, Robbie found a man whom he could trust. His kind face, his good sentiments, his position in the world, his apparent indifference to a sum like five thousand dollars, his absorbing passion for horses, his knowledge of them, his elegance of manner, his ease and grace of language, his liberal but sincere flattery, his dress, his generous invitation to dine with him, his condescension, his attentiveness, captured Robbie completely. It never occurred to him that his new friend had acted in a highly eccentric manner; that his conduct was not that of a practical, hard-headed business man. On the contrary, Robbie regarded the judge as one of a type of which the world was full, and he fondly imagined that all of his business in the future would be with men like S. P. Bowers. For fairness, for honesty, for goodness, he even placed him above his Uncle Phineas, whom he had always regarded till now as the most perfect man on earth.

"Surely," he thought, "the world is full of good men." Phineas Strong was the first one he had ever met; Judge Bowers was the last. He did not think of this now, but it came to him in after years.

CHAPTER XXV.

AT five o'clock, Judge Bowers, Robbie Porter and Dewy Iris were passengers on the Baltimore steamer, and it was moving gracefully from the landing to the middle of the Rappahannock. Robbie and his friend stood upon the upper deck aft of the ladies' saloon.

"It was about at this spot," said Robbie, "that we crossed the river on December 12, 1862, under General French."

"And did you see the battle of Fredericksburg?" queried the judge.

"I was in it."

"In it?"

"Yes, sir!"

"Why, what do you mean?"

"Carried a drum, and beat it in every charge up Marye's Heights yonder. Went up six times, and came back, and that's more than many can say. My father, sir, carried the company's colors, and once got it planted on a rebel battery. He was knocked down with a gun, and the flag thrown after him. I picked it up, and waved it till pap got his breath, and then we were ordered to retreat. I could have walked back to the river on dead soldiers, but as we all ran pretty fast, I often fell down between them. Pap lost the colors—

staff and flag shot to fragments; lost his cap; a piece of shell cut off his left trouser leg just below the knee as nice as you could have done it with shears; another knocked the heel and nearly all the sole off of his right shoe, and a minie ball bored a hole through my right leg, the marks of which are still to be seen. My shoe was full of blood when we were ordered to halt. Pap answered to roll call that night, and I stood by his side!"

"Merciful Heavens!" said the judge; "and you saw all that? Why, you must have been a child!"

"About twelve!"

"And they allowed you in battle?"

"No, sir. They didn't allow it, but I was in it. Wherever pap went, I went. I ran away when he enlisted, and followed him through the war—till——"

"Till when?"

"Till he was killed at Chancellorsville," said Robbie, suppressing the emotion which the recollection of the event seemed momentarily to cause.

"My only son," said the judge, "lost his life in the battle of Fredericksburg. He was a lieutenant in the Ninety-seventh Pennsylvania Volunteers, and was among the first to fall."

"Many a brave man went down that day, never to rise again!" sympathetically replied the boy. "Why, Burnside lost thirteen thousand men in that battle!"

"Awful, sir, awful!" said the judge. "And to think of you being a witness—being in it, why, sir, you are a hero;—and did your leg get well?"

"Oh, yes! Didn't bother me much. Bathed it that night in the cold waters of the river, tied it up with rags, and carried the same drum for four days in the battle of Chancellorsville. There it was filled full of bullet holes, and so broken that I had to let it go."

"And were you injured in that battle?"

"Oh, only knocked down a few times. My father, however, received a wound on the last day that caused his death the day after, from loss of blood."

"Terrible! Awful! Awful!" said the judge. "And were you in other battles?"

"That was the last one, but I was in ten battles; and I guess I have seen ten thousand dead soldiers!"

"Is it possible? You don't say so!"

"Yes!" went on Robbie, "and our armies were whipped in every one of them. We had brave soldiers, but poor generals."

"How about McClellan?"

"He was great on a retreat."

"Well, you know the old saying,

> " ' He who fights and runs away,
>   May live to fight another day.' "

"I've heard that; but my experience is that

> " ' He who fights and runs away,
>   Is *afraid* to fight another day.' "

"Well, now," said the judge, laughing, "there may be something in that; but the Union generals *won* some battles."

"Didn't win any that I saw. They were too slow. Lee and Jackson generally got us on the run before they stopped fighting!"

"How about Gettysburg?"

"I didn't see that fight," said Robbie, "but from what I have heard about it, the Confederates did the fighting and the Union army the resisting!"

"But it was called a great victory by General Meade."

"Well," said Robbie, "if I should try and throw you overboard, and you, by getting behind the rail there, and hanging on to the ropes, should thwart my purpose, I suppose you could go home and tell about your victory; but if in saving yourself, you succeeded in killing me, or tossing me overboard, you would feel more like claiming a victory, would you not?"

"To be sure," said the judge; "but many of the Southerners *were* killed!"

"True, but we lost twenty-three thousand men; the Confederates twenty thousand, and Lee was allowed to escape by Meade, just as McClellan suffered him to do at Antietam. Had Grant commanded at either place he would have annihilated the Confederate army."

"Why, you don't think Grant a great general, do you?" asked the judge in a surprised tone. "I regard him as a merciless butcher!"

"Some day," said Robbie, "when a calmer judgment makes up the verdict, the greatest military hero of the last war will be conceded to be Ulysses S. Grant. He is greater than Cæsar, greater than Hannibal, greater than Alexander, greater than Frederick, greater than Napoleon, greater than Wellington. He fought, or directed, sixty-eight battles in the war and won them all. Measured by his successes, he is the greatest military genius that ever lived in any clime or in any age. He never stopped fighting as long as there was anything to fight, and he is the only general in all history that never lost a battle. Some day, sir, his monument will pierce the clouds."

"I admire your frankness," said the judge, "but don't indorse your sentiments. At any rate, it was a glorious war, and it did a great thing for humanity!"

"There was a time, sir, when I so thought; but now, I am convinced that Glory was the only redeeming part of the war!"

"But, sir, it preserved the Union, and abolished slavery."

"Yes, that it did those two things," replied Robbie, "I am willing to concede; but of just what particular benefit those things are to you or me, or even to the freed slave, I have, I confess, never been able to see."

"Why, you astonish me," said the judge. "No benefit to preserve the Union; no benefit to abolish slavery? Why, surely, young man, you cannot, you do not mean that?"

"The Union," replied Robbie, "because of the diversity of interests, of tastes and customs, will some day be dismembered, and what is now apparently a restored and harmonized Republic will some day be a half-dozen kingdoms or republics. The slave is worse off in his freedom, more ragged, more helpless, more immoral, than ever he was in his bondage. Sentiment made him free, but sentiment does not employ him nor support him. Men who laid down their lives for him on the field of battle, would not, if they now lived, admit him to either their tables or their beds. Besides, sir, the war has literally ruined one-third of the Republic, and for the next thirty years its effects will keep the South, with all its natural and abundant resources, on the verge of poverty. The bitterness engendered by fraternal strife will continue for generations; for fifty years to come, in words and thoughts, the war will be fought over and over again. In my judgment the war was worse than slavery; worse than a dismembered Union. 'Glory,' said Sir Walter Scott, 'is the faded hatchment that hangs over the warrior's dim and moldering tomb,' but that is the only consolation the war has left to the survivors of the victims!"

At this speech, delivered by Robbie with the enthusiasm of youth and the vehemence of the truth he felt, Judge Bowers was very much surprised. He did not attempt a reply; but observing that the night air was chilly, begged to be excused for the evening. Requesting Robbie to look after the horses, and share the upper berth of his stateroom, the good man pleasantly withdrew.

CHAPTER XXVI.

ROBBIE, after wondering for a moment if he had offended the judge, and wishing that he had been more guarded, proceeded to the lower deck and carefully inspected his charges.   Giving each a bunch of hay, he proceeded to examine every part of the boat.   This completed, he entered the stateroom occupied by his friend, and heard him read as he opened the door:

"And John beheld a white horse."

"Just in time," said the judge.   "Always read a chapter in the Bible before I retire.   Wonderful book, is the Bible.   Do you read the Bible?   Good church-goer, I hope, and a Christian?"

To these queries Robbie made no haste to reply. Not liking to offend his friend, as he was afraid he might should he answer truthfully, he at first was inclined to be evasive; but reflecting that for the next year this man would no doubt see him daily, he concluded that he had better be frank.   Therefore, looking the judge full and fair in the face he said:

"I have read some of the Bible, but I have never read it through.   I have not, to my knowledge, ever been in a place of worship.   In a correct sense, I am not a Christian."

"But you believe the Bible? believe in Revelation? Believe on the Lord Jesus Christ?"

"To be fair, sir, I am afraid I believe in neither or none of these things."

Judge Bowers dropped his book and stared: "Don't believe!" he said. "Don't believe that Jesus died for us! My dear young man, have you a Bible? None, I dare say! Well, I'll buy you one to-morrow; read it, my boy, read it. You are too intelligent not to be impressed. It will open your eyes, and show you how to avoid hell and attain heaven."

"Of heaven or hell," said Robbie, "I also know nothing. At present no reason for the existence of either appears to me. I would abolish both. If the object of heaven is happiness, man may be happy here. If the purpose of hell is punishment, man may be punished here. It is repugnant to my ideas that man can be so bad that God will punish him forever in hell. Nor do I conceive that a God, however wise and good, can create a place where eternal or perfect happiness may exist. Something, some time, would happen and some misery would prevail. My idea is to so live while here that I will avoid punishment and attain happiness. To my mind any scheme of religion that fails to help us in this is a failure. I very much question any plan, the chief purpose of which is to assure benefits beyond the grave, for I am now fully persuaded that the capacity to enjoy after death is very limited."

"The spirit, my dear boy, the spirit is that which lives and suffers, or is happy. You have an immortal soul that never dies."

"This," said Robbie, "I have often heard before, but

the reason, or argument for it, I have never been able to appreciate.''

"But you want to live forever, don't you?''

"As to what I want,'' replied Robbie, "will not alter the fact, nor solve the question. When for me life has lost its charm, I imagine I would rather die. What the rest of mankind may desire can in no manner affect me. My personal opinion, which it seems you desire I should express on the subject, is that man has no soul, no spirit, as you call it, and that when he dies, his consciousness dies also. To quote from the Book whose perusal you so earnestly recommend: 'There is no knowledge, nor wisdom, nor device in the grave whither thou goest. For that which befalleth the sons of men befalleth beasts; even one thing befalleth them; as the one dieth, so dieth the other; yea, they have all one breath; so that a man hath no pre-eminence above a beast: for all is vanity. All go unto one place, all are of the dust, and all turn to dust again.' ''

The judge was not only shocked but nearly dumfounded. He deplored Robbie's lost condition, promised that on the morrow he would explain the passage just quoted, and concluded the evening by reading the thirteenth chapter of Corinthians.

As Robbie lay there in his berth, listening to the sighing wind and hearing now and then the splashing waves against the steamer's sides, these words of the chapter kept ringing in his ears:

"Though I speak with the tongues of men and of angels, and have not charity, I am become as a sounding brass and as a tinkling cymbal; and though I have the gift of prophecy, and understand all mysteries and all knowledge, and though I have all faith so that I could remove mountains, and have not charity, I am nothing."

He fell asleep, deeply impressed with the beauty of the words.   When he awoke, the paddle wheels of the steamer were stirring up the aromatic mud that forms the bed of the Patapsco River.

CHAPTER XXVII.

MOUNTED upon Dewy Iris, and leading by her side the two brood mares, Robbie made his way from the landing along one of the crowded streets of Baltimore. Judge Bowers proceeded on foot a little in advance, and directed the way. Arrived at the freight depot, arrangements for the transportation of the horses, with Robbie as attendant, were completed. They were placed carefully and securely in a car. One end Robbie arranged for himself. Hay, oats, and a barrel of water were supplied, and to his surprise and delight Judge Bowers announced his intention of accompanying Robbie and the horses in the car. It being nearly noon, and the train being scheduled to depart at six, and both gentlemen being hungry, they repaired to a modest eating house. Completing his meal, Robbie signified his intention of seeing something of the city. To this proposition the judge assented, requesting him to be at the car before six, where, said his good-natured and good-hearted friend: "I will have a blanket for myself, and a Bible for you, a box to sit on, a candle to give light, and a lunch to eat. Don't get lost, and be careful."

Robbie had proceeded a little distance when a placard, on which was written, "Four tintypes for fifty cents," attracted his attention. He entered the photographer's and sat for his picture. This done, and the four tin-types in his possession, he immediately selected what he conceived the best reproduction; bought of the operator an envelope and a sheet of paper. On the former he wrote:

"PHŒBE STRONG,
"Richardsville,
"Culpepper Co., Va."

On the latter this:

"DEAREST PHŒBE: Just arrived in Baltimore. Met in Fredericksburg a Judge Bowers, of Lancaster, Pa. He has bought Dewy Iris for five thousand dollars. He has paid me two thousand dollars, and will pay me the balance on the day within a year that I drive Dewy Iris a mile in harness in two minutes and eighteen seconds. As I once drove her in two minutes and fifteen seconds on the big road, thee can see that I am certain of the money, unless Dewy Iris dies. I am to live with the judge during the time and have charge of her. I am to have my board, and be allowed to go to school, in exchange for my services in caring for and driving Iris.

"This judge, Phœbe, is nice looking, educated, refined, generous, about sixty-eight, rich, and has two hobbies—the Bible and race horses. He knows the former from cover to cover, and the name of every trotting horse from Ariel to General Taylor, and from George M. Patchen to Dexter and Flora Temple. He claims to own the fastest horses in Pennsylvania.

"Dearest, sweetest Phœbe, I will study hard, and

will come back and we will be married in the Quaker
way, with just Uncle Phineas and Aunt Rachel for
witnesses.   Give my love to them; remember me to all
the help.   Phœbe, I am going to study law, and get to
be a judge.   I enclose my picture.   Please, Phœbe,
get some taken when thee is next in Fredericksburg
and send one to me, so that I may always have before
my eyes the face of one whose image is ever in my
mind, and whose affection I hope always to possess.

"Oh, Phœbe, I cannot write my love, but thee, thee
knows it!   It will outlive the tongue that thus feebly
tries to express it.   My heart beats quicker when I
think of thee, and as thee is seldom out of my thoughts,
my heart is always thumping against my ribs.   Write
to me, Phœbe.   Write to me at once.   I am not, after
all, far away, and, in spirit, be assured, I will still
clasp thy hand, and always be within the sound of
the music of thy voice.   Farewell, sweet love.   The
memory of thy goodness will be the inspiration of my
life, and in the end help me to the last round in the
ladder of fame.

"Thine ever loving,
"ROBBIE.

"Address
      "Care JUDGE BOWERS,
                "Lancaster, Pa.''

This written, and inclosed with the tintype, was,
after much inquiry, deposited in the post office, and
Robbie strolled about the city.   It was Wednesday.
The clouds had all disappeared, and the November
sun shone clear and warm.

Attracted by a crowd of gayly dressed people, princi-
pally ladies, who seemed to be struggling for admission

to a large building, he also drew near, and from a sign which adorned one side of the entrance, he learned that the place was a theater, and that a performance would take place that afternoon. The play announced was the "Lady of Lyons."

In a Fifth Reader at River View Robbie had read an extract from this very play. A desire to read it all had long been cherished. Here was an opportunity that might never again be enjoyed. He could not only hear the piece repeated, but could behold the impersonations of the characters, and witness the passionate, pathetic scenes between Claude and Pauline. The size and elegance of the crowd urging admittance argued not only the popularity of the piece, but the genius of those who were to present it. Following the line, therefore, he was soon face to face with the ticket seller. Much to his surprise he was told that all seats were sold, that only standing room could be had. The crush was now so great that a man appeared and announced in a loud voice that the house was full, and no more admissions for that performance would be taken. The ticket seller closed his window. Those whose forethought had induced them to purchase tickets in advance continued smilingly to enter the place, while the others, frowning and pouting, slowly and sullenly turned away. Robbie joined the latter, feeling rather disappointed.

He had reached the sidewalk when a man approached and asked him if he would like to purchase a seat for the performance. Inasmuch as he had just heard the

seats were all sold, the query was not a little surprising.
The man, however, assured him that he had actually
one seat in an upper box of which he wished to dispose.
He offered it for four dollars, saying that it had cost
him five. It was an extravagant and unheard-of price,
yet I think Robbie would have parted just then with
double the sum, so keen was his desire to see the play.
He, therefore, fearing some one else would offer more,
produced four dollars, secured the coveted ticket, and
in a few moments, just as the curtain was rising, was
led into a box, beautifully decorated, hung with silken
curtains, furnished with upholstered chairs, and already
partly occupied by three ladies; two young, very pretty,
and richly dressed; the third, middle-aged, dressed
in black, gray-haired, pleasant in face, and perfect in
feature. What they thought at the entrance of Robbie,
I am not prepared to say. What they looked plainly
indicated displeasure. The noses of the three turned
up perceptibly, and the two young ladies deliberately
turned their backs to our hero. One drew her skirts
close to her chair, as he took the vacant seat at her side.

Robbie wore neither collar nor tie. His hair was
long and fell in waves and curls around his neck and
over his coat collar. His trousers were tucked into the
legs of his top boots. His coat was plain, vest and
trousers of the same material, good, but of a style and
make suggestive of long ago. His brown hat, crushed
and mud-stained, rested idly in his bare, rough hands,
and from his person I have no doubt there floated a well-
defined aroma of Dewy Iris!

Upon the rising curtain and the brilliant scene around him Robbie was already intent.

What a magnificent spectacle of bewildering gowns and bright faces. The *élite* and fashion of all Baltimore were before him. There were the Misses Garretts, and there the Misses Reynolds. In one box were the Passmores, and in another the Fultons. The rich Supplesses and the powerful Latrobes were all represented in that gorgeous galaxy of rich costumes and animated, expectant countenances.

It was indeed a testimonial to one of Baltimore's beautiful daughters, once, and then, a petted idol, and the most charming of all the impersonators of Pauline.

The house was heavy with the perfume of roses. The beautiful Pauline, in the person of Katie Bateman; —yes, it was no less than the divine, the sylph-like, the young, the brilliant Katie Bateman, who had already heard the tumultuous plaudits of kings and princes, lords and dukes, queens and duchesses;—no sooner made her appearance, than the whole house began such a clapping of hands as to stop her speech, while around her fell a shower of roses that for a moment concealed from the eyes of her admiring audience her lovely form.

And, reader, if thou hast never seen Katie Bateman, thou hast never seen a real impassioned Pauline. This day she seemed to play the part with even greater vigor and sweeter grace than ever before. Her Claude was, I think, Lester Wallack, but of that Robbie was never quite certain. To Pauline, however, his attention was given entirely. He fancied she was Phœbe, and imagined himself as the low-born gardener's son, who had feasted for years upon the object of his passion, till at last her "image had become glassed in his soul," and he could no longer resist the impulses of his heart.

How this play impressed itself upon the mind of this Virginia country boy! How absorbed he became; how real to him were all the scenes, all the situations; how he longed for an eloquence like Claude; and how he resolved, ere the performance had concluded, to join the army, hope for another *war*—"just one more," he thought, so that he might win a dozen battles, and return with epaulets, a shining sword, a brilliant coat, and lead his graceful Phœbe forth to the musical marches of a minuet, in a magnificent ballroom, where every tongue would praise his prowess and every eye would follow his form. He would feel at last that he was worthy of even so perfect, so divine, so good a creature as his noble Phœbe.

"But, alas!" he thought, "Phœbe hated war, and, perhaps, after all, he could do something besides kill men in battle, and be just as great as being a general in the army."

But the play and its chief character he never forgot. The Quaker prejudices of the theater, which for more than seven years he had been taught to cultivate, faded away, never to return. In their place came a love and admiration for the playhouse that grew and flourished as time advanced. He left the theater regretting that he could not upon canvas immortalize the beauty of this favored young actress. Tradition, however, has preserved the memory of her achievements, and literature, in a measure, added additional luster to her name. It was his hope that she, and hundreds of others whom he saw in after years, might preserve by their power and their dignity the beauty and the charm that linger around the stage. Happy in their chosen work, enthused and intoxicated with the tumult of popular applause, may they yet, like Miss Bateman, become and remain virtuous wives and noble mothers, and under the summer skies of happiness, move onward to the shining sea, Success.

Robbie departed, charmed with the entertainment, and bewildered by its brilliant assemblage. He had forgotten his plain costume, his gloveless hands, and collarless neck. He was in a dream. He only awoke when he entered the freight car where the horses were, and heard Judge Bowers read:

"And I John beheld a white horse!"

CHAPTER XXVIII.

AND what, after all, a character this man Bowers seemed to be. All of his failings leaned to virtue's side, and hence he was odd. He continually attracted attention and excited remark. He would quote a passage from the Bible, and slide gracefully from its sacred pages to the trotting record of Captain McGowan, General Butler, Dexter, or Julia Aldrich.

He was now seated upon a soap box, and by the aid of a tallow-candle light, reading a passage of Holy Writ. While Robbie loitered at the theater, the judge had been industrious. In a corner of the car, with the aid of the hay, and some newly purchased horse blankets, he had arranged two very inviting beds. Upon another soap box he had spread a large pie, a segment of yellow cheese, some fresh rolls, a jar of milk, a can of raw oysters, a paper of salt, another of pepper, and an iron, two-tined fork. On one end of the box, and near the pie lay a brand-new Bible, in a black, expensive binding.

"There!" said the judge, as he laid down his book, took off his glasses, and wiped them, "I expect that is the greatest book ever written. My friend, I have taken the liberty to buy you a volume. I have written your name in it, as a present from me. Accept it, and promise me you will read it through. Commence to-night, and read it every night as long as you live. Will you promise to read every word of it?"

"I will," replied Robbie.

"Well, give the horses their suppers and eat your own. We'll be starting soon. There's a cask of water near Dewy Iris—what a wonder she'll be—Dexter and the Dutchman will fade from the history of the turf after next August."

Here he broke out with: "When the roll is called up yonder, I'll be there," etc.

Robbie fed the horses, ate his supper, and was just beginning to gather up the fragments of the feast, when the car suddenly started, precipitating Robbie, pie, cheese, Bible and the judge upon the floor.

No damage was done, other than extinguishing the light. Another was soon obtained, the door made secure, and Robbie proceeded to examine his present.

"That's right; that's right!" said the judge, though the noise of the grinding wheels compelled him to elevate his voice to a high pitch. "Start right in. Seems strange that a bright, well-read boy like you never read the Bible. You say your uncle raised you?"

"Yes, sir!" Robbie answered.

"And never compelled you to read the Bible, never taught you to pray?" went on the judge.

"No, he never did."

"And what kind of a man was he?"

"If," said Robbie, "I should tell you of his character, I am sure you would admit that a man might be good without religion, and might be posted without reading the Bible."

."What was his character?"

"Well, to borrow from Mr. Goldsmith, 'he was an husbandman, and the father of a family.' He was just in all his dealings, generous and brave in his impulses, frank and open in his expressions, sincere and warm in his friendships, affectionate and considerate in all of his domestic relations, calm in his demeanor, correct in his conclusions, right in his judgments, genial in his temper, sweet in his disposition, good to the poor, envied not the rich, broad in his views, clean in his person, faultless in his attire, the debtor to no man, paid his taxes promptly, loaned his money to all who applied, and took neither interest nor security, lived justly and plainly, talked honestly, gave to every man his own, freed his slaves twenty years before the war broke out, gave four sons to the cause of the Union, never swore an oath, never drank a drop of liquor, never used tobacco, scorned a lie, and loved the truth; was rock and oak, or vine and flower, as occasion required, never struck a child nor whipped his horses, visited the widow and the fatherless in their affliction, worshipped the quality of mercy, opened his hand and his doors to the needy, sought no public office, fed and clothed both the enemies and defenders of his country, paid homage to his wife——"

"Stop! stop!" said the judge. "Was there, is there, such a character?"

"There *is* such a character, and his name is Phineas ·

Strong, and from such a man I have conceived some of my notions of life!"

"And how high," inquired the judge, "will his monument be when he dies?"

"So high!" said Robbie, with emphasis, "that its peak will pierce the clouds!"

"Good! good!" cried the judge. "You would make a splendid lawyer. You should study law."

"I will," said Robbie, "and I will begin under you!"

"I wish you a better tutor," laughingly replied the judge. "But it is hard work to talk, so, suppose you read a chapter in the Bible—your eyes are brighter than mine—I'll pray, and we will compose ourselves to sleep!"

"All right," said Robbie; "what chapter shall I read?"

"Any one! Any one! They are all good! Can't get one that I don't approve, unless it is that one which has in it 'Put not you trust in horses!' Read from the Old Testament!"

Robbie opened the book at random, and started to read the thirty-eighth chapter of Genesis. He had proceeded about half through, innocently and unexpectedly, when he happened to stop and glance at the judge. His face was something of a study. He looked a trifle annoyed and considerably perplexed.

"Wouldn't finish that chapter to-night!" he spoke. "Let's have a little prayer and retire. Will be in Lancaster early.

Robbie, however, was anxious to finish the chapter,

and as the judge kneeled and prayed, he concluded its perusal. Its contents were a revelation, and perhaps, reader, they will be to you.

Judge Bowers talked him to sleep trying to explain how it was necessary to employ inspiration to tell a story like that about Judah's and his daughter-in-law.

When he awoke the car was being pulled into the city of Lancaster.

CHAPTER XXIX.

AT this time Lancaster contained more than twenty thousand people. It was then, as now, an active, bustling place. Iron furnaces day and night sent lurid blasts of flame and clouds of smoke to the sky. The noise of the shuttle and the clang of the loom could be heard in many quarters, and from more than one hundred warehouses the flavor of the tobacco leaf floated out upon the air. The imposing courthouse and the tall tower of the sinister jail loomed before the eyes of the visitor. Franklin and Marshall Colleges invited those who would worship at the shrine of Minerva.

The city is regularly laid out, on the banks of the Conestoga River, which supplies water power to its numerous mills. There were many substantial and elegant homes in Lancaster, even then, and among the most attractive and most inviting, at least in its exterior appearance, in a retired, well shaded street, in a quiet part of the city, was that occupied by Judge Bowers, and toward which our hero, Dewy Iris, the two mares, and the judge himself were now very closely approached.

"Here we are! Here we are! Home at last!" exclaimed the judge, as he showed Robbie and his charges through a double iron gate that led to the driveway to the barn in the rear of the house.

It was a large square, brick barn, handsomely finished in and out. Producing a key, the judge soon unlocked a door, and entering, opened double doors, and Dewy Iris was soon quartered in a roomy box stall of her own.

"Now," said the judge, "here is the key to that stall. No one shall enter it but you. Into your hands, sir, I commit the mare. You are to feed her, groom her, drive her. In consideration of which, you are to make your home with me, dine at my table, be my guest, my honored guest, sir, till next August, and longer, if we are all agreeable. All that I require of you is the proper care of that animal, which I know you are competent to bestow. The rest of the time is your own—to read, to study, to go to school, or do what you like. Is it a bargain?"

"It is a bargain!" answered Robbie. "And, further, not that you have forgotten it, on the day within a year that I drive Dewy Iris one mile on the Lancaster County track, in less than two minutes and eighteen seconds, you will hand me three thousand dollars in money, and the check for two thousand dollars?"

"That is the agreement," said the judge.

"And if I fail, you will accept the mare for a year's board?" asked Robbie.

"If you fail," said the judge, "I will give you two thousand dollars, and keep the mare. I know, however, that the mare will wake up a sleeping world, and will do pretty near what you say. The check, sir, I will leave at the bank to-day, subject to your order. Consider that yours, no matter what happens.''

"Let us shake hands," said Robbie.

The two men immediately clasped hands. They then proceeded along a stone walk to the house.

This house occupied, and perhaps still occupies, a large, well-shaded lawn, sloping on all sides to the walls of a stone fence, capped with granite flags and adorned with a low iron fence, painted black. It was full two stories, of brick, with a quadrangular built roof, converging toward a center at the peak, which was surmounted with a cupola. It had four tall chimneys of brick, one on either corner. It was flanked on all sides by wide porches, whose roofs were supported by filagree pillars of iron. It had four entrances, exactly in the center of its sides, and four wide halls. In the basement was a large kitchen, and on the first floor were four large apartments. One of these, lighted by four tall windows, was the judge's library, a room of spacious dimensions and lofty ceiling. Into this Robbie was now ushered.

It being early, these two were the only ones about the premises that were stirring. A coal fire, not very bright, burned upon the hearth. Before this, the judge seated our hero, and excused himself, saying he would go and arouse the household. He therefore departed, and Robbie began a quiet inspection of the room and its contents. Opening the shutters to receive more light, his eyes fell upon a scene which filled him with delight.

The room, on its four sides, contained cases, some of which reached to the ceiling, and were filled with books —books, beautifully bound, richly marked.

Above him, and occupying nearly all the space of the chimney over the mantel, in a magnificent frame of gilt, hung an oil painting, the spirit, life and color of which held him spellbound.   It was the "Horse Fair." done by no less a genius than the noted Rosa Bonheur.   I am not prepared to say that this was the original of that famous painting   A. T. Stewart, of New York, once owned it, and it was about this time that this great work of the artist was sold in the United States for ten thousand dollars.

To Robbie it appeared the grandest picture he ever saw, and no doubt it was.   Occupying a similar space on the opposite wall hung a painting of "Christ Before Pilate," far less attractive than the picture of the horses.   The walls were further adorned with colored prints of Flora Temple, Dexter, General Butler, and other famous trotting kings of the turf in harness, and pictured as leading the race in the stretch on some race track, while a multitude of beholders threw their hats in the air.

It was, however, to the books that Robbie cast his most tender glances.   He found one case that struck him at once as highly reflective of the character of its owner.   Side by side, reposing calmly and contentedly were Baxter's "Saint's Rest," a copy of "The English Stud Book," by Messrs. Weatherby; "Divine Revelation," by Fox; the "Racing Calendar," De Witte's

"Einlitung," Whyte's "History of the Turf," Tregelles on "The Texts of the New Testament," Mayhew on "The Management of the Horse," Hitchcock's "Analysis of the Bible," Percival's "Anatomy of the Horse," "The Atonement," by Dr. A. A. Hodge, "The American Trotting Register," "Festivals and Fasts," by Bishop Hobart, and bound volumes of *The Spirit of the Times*. These books, and some venerable law volumes, gave external evidence of having been frequently consulted.

But there were at least two thousand others, fresh and nearly new, among which, in cloth and gold, he beheld the matchless novels of Fielding, the rare romances of Scott, the beauties of Bulwer, and indeed, a whole realm of fiction and history, law, religion, politics, biography and poetry. There was a classic collection, which included Herodotus, Apulieus, Sallust, Ovid, Homer, Pliny, Josephus, his beloved Virgil, Cicero, and a dozen others, all of which he was trying to inspect at one and the same time, when the sound of voices arrested his attention. He heard, in rather animated tones:

"Just like you, always bringing some tramp or clodhopper to the house!"

"But, my dear! I am sure you misjudge the young man!"

"Misjudge nothing! I know you too well. But I'll not stand it longer. He shall just pack up and be off. Pay him for his horse, and tell him so, or I will; I'll have no more paupers in the house!"

"He shall at least breakfast here."

This Robbie recognized as the voice of Judge Bowers, who at that moment, somewhat red in the face, and evidently embarrassed, entered the room.

"Breakfast will be ready soon, and while they are getting it, I'll show you your room!" he observed, Robbie imagined, rather timidly.

The judge led the way to the second floor and showed his guest into a large rear room, elegantly furnished. There were pictures on the walls, and a writing desk in one corner. The carpet was of velvet, Robbie thought, four inches thick.

"Just make yourself at home. Find soap and towels, brush and comb, and fix yourself up a bit. Bell rings once, then come down." With this he left.

Robbie could hardly believe his senses. He had never seen anything like this in his life. He was afraid to sit down or touch a thing lest he soil it. However he soon found some sweet-scented soap and with its aid, water, brush and comb, made himself presentable. Without waiting for the bell, he descended the stairs and had approached the library when more loud talking arrested him. A woman's voice said:

"And you gave him the best spare room? Sam Bowers! I do think you've lost your senses! I've a good mind not to eat with you!"

Robbie felt, uneasily, that he was the subject of these and the former remarks, and that the owner of the voice was no doubt Mrs. Bowers. His face burned with indignation, and he was about ready to depart the house, fully convinced that his further continuance would cause both the judge and his wife great domestic difference, when a door before him opened and the lady herself suddenly appeared.

Robbie looked confused, and Mrs. Bowers, for she it was, colored to the roots of her hair. Instinctively she knew, and her face expressed it, that she had been overheard. The mutual embarrassment lasted nearly a minute. The lady was the first to speak. She smiled on Robbie, and remarked, rather sarcastically he thought, "Mr. Porter, I believe—the judge's friend?"

"Yes," said Robbie, still under the influence of the indignation and mortification of the situation.

"Permit me," said the lady, really in a condescending tone, "to show you to the breakfast room!" She opened the very door through which she had just emerged, indicating by a motion of her rather heavily jeweled hand that she expected him to follow her. This he did, no doubt largely influenced by the flavor of a warm breakfast that floated into his nostrils, and intensified his already large desire to eat.

The judge, who was seated by a window, arose as the two entered, and said:

"My wife, Mr. Porter. Josephine, this is Mr. Robert Porter, who is to be our guest for the next year!"

The lady not only bowed gracefully, but smiled also as she acknowledged the introduction, and actually said (bless the sex!): "Delighted to meet you, Mr. Porter; charmed to welcome you. I hope you will like Lancaster."

For the life of him Robbie could not determine whether the lady was joking or in earnest. He was inclined to conclude the former, but she had extended her hand with such promptness, and clasped his own with such evident sincerity, that all of his resentment vanished, and he was quite willing to forgive her hasty remarks. The truth was, that Mrs. Bowers, having had an opportunity to survey Robbie from head to foot, had, in spite of his rural appearance, in spite of his top boots and rather crude manners, undergone a complete change of sentiment.

She was agreeably surprised, for reader, our hero already possessed, physically, parts calculated to charm a woman. He was now well grown, five feet nine or ten inches; with a well-shaped head, covered with a wealth of brown curls that fell gracefully around his neck; a high, smooth forehead, blue eyes, large, tender and frank, beaming with the glance of innocence; cheeks flushed with the color of health, red lips, a dimpled chin, broad shoulders; straight as an arrow—all of his movements indicating the athlete and the elasticity of youth.

The soap and water recently applied had removed the traces of the night's journey, and the soap had left a polished luster on face and brow; so, in all, he presented a more attractive picture to the lady than she had prepared herself to view. Therefore her hand had been extended with genuine regard, and her voice was intended to reflect what was now the real sentiment of her mind.

Before the breakfast concluded she was all graciousness, not only to her husband but to Robbie. She laughed, joked, and openly apologized for her unkind remarks about the new guest. Begged Robbie to forgive her, saying, as an excuse, that Mr. Bowers had long been in the habit of bringing irresponsible people and orphan boys into the house, and all of them had been ungrateful, some dishonest, many dirty and ignorant, so that she was compelled to "put her foot down," as she expressed it, and read the law to Mr. Bowers.

She had all of Robbie's sympathy, and all of his confidence before they left the room. She told him she was a farmer's daughter, and always liked farmers' boys until she met the judge, and had only agreed to marry him on being satisfied that he was once a plowman.

"Well," said Robbie, "it has been often observed, that a plowman on his feet is better than a gentleman on his knees!"

"Good! good!" exclaimed the judge, and they arose from the table.

CHAPTER XXX.

JUDGE BOWERS was then among the most prominent citizens of Lancaster. For nearly thirty years he had been a judge, a politician, a lover of fast horses, and a leader in the social and religious life of the town. He was rich in purse, lands and learning. Of a pure mind, a generous heart, and a pleasing disposition, he had warm friends among a wide acquaintance. His home was among the most elegant, his library the largest, his wife the handsomest, and his horses the fastest. He was trusted by all who knew him; had no enemies, and was envied by all the world as a happy man.

He was not.

His present matrimonial partner was his second. She was about forty years his junior. They had been married nearly ten years. They had no children; and generally found their chief source of happiness in social display, or church charities. They had long become conspicuous for both.

The heart of the wife had never yet been touched by the sweetness of love, and the heart of the husband was long since dead to its influences. These two, therefore, lived together without passion or sentiment. Their domestic differences were many, but never loud or vio-

lent.   The natural refinement of the judge, and a sense
of policy on the part of the wife, prevented open rup-
tures, and so they lived together, in the eyes of the
world, amicably and even happy.   At church, in the
social throng, in public court, in the presence of guests,
these two smiled upon and "deared" each other with
all the enthusiasm of real love, and employed those
melting, tender expressions genuine passion only in-
spires.   Alone, however, they rarely spoke, and in the
solitude of their own bed chamber, each turned back to
back.   The memories of the past soothed into sleep the
hapless husband, while dreams of the future revelled in
the ambitious brain of the wife.   For it was ambition
that induced Josephine Hessing to become Mrs. Judge
Bowers.

She was the daughter of a farmer near Millersville,
whose ancestry was Dutch.   She inherited many of the
Dutch characteristics.   She had been passably educated,
religiously brought up, and up to this time had conducted herself as the dignified wife of a rich judge
should.   Her conduct had always been discreet and
womanly.   She stood high in the church, was a regular communicant, sipped the wine and broke the bread
with closed eyes, devout and penitent expression.   At
social functions she outshone, outdressed all of her
former schoolgirl companions, and yet her graciousness was such that even her lady friends spoke of her
character with approbation.   Her generous donations
to the church and to the unfortunate, made her name
generally known and highly revered.

She, however, married Judge Bowers because his
notice of her beauty flattered her, and because everybody said it was a splendid match. Well, she got a
full purse, to be sure, but she had to be content with
an empty heart!

She now owned to twenty-eight years; being devout,
the reader will not question her age. She was as tall,
if not taller, than Robbie; her form was perfect in its
outline, properly proportioned as to bust and waist,
more inclined to *embonpoint* than to spare. Her head
was shapely, and crowned with an abundance of light
brown hair, which she usually dressed into a pompadour
roll in front, and gathered into a net in the rear. Her
eyes were of medium size, steel gray, and not without
an expression of tenderness. All of her features were
exactly regular; her nose straight, with wide nostrils,
pink and thin. Over her entire face the glow of perfect health suffused itself. Her lips, of course, while
they were red, and curved so as to indicate a pleasant
disposition, were perhaps hardly thin enough to be
classic or cold, and hardly thick enough to indicate
warmth or affection. Her teeth were well preserved,
remarkably white, regular, and evidently the subject of
much care. She smiled as she talked, and her smile
invited your confidence. Her chin was rounded, and
as not therefore strictly classical. Her hands were
small, full of rings, and her fingers tapered.

Her costume, on the morning Robbie first beheld her,
was a loose-fitting garment—a wrapper, with a watteau
pleat down the back, and a train that swept the floor.

It was of a warm, wool material, deep maroon in color, fastened about her neck by means of a gold pin, and gathered about her waist and held in place by means of a belt. Whenever she moved her arms, a delicate scent, like lilac, floated from her person, and brought back to our hero a memory of the delicious flowers that flourished on the terraces of his Virginia home.

Into this place, and in the companionship of these two people, Robbie Porter was to pass the next year of his life. As he immeditately completed arrangements for entering a private academy near by, he soon found that in his efforts to read all of the books in Judge Bowers' library, to keep up his school duties, and to give to Dewy Iris that care and attention which a great trotting animal requires, he had little time for sleep or social enjoyment.

He sometimes sat down at night to read, and read till breakfast. In a few months he knew more about the books in the house and their contents than the judge himself. It was here he read Voltaire's "Philosophical Dictionary," Bishop Colenso's "Pentateuch," Thomas Paine's "Age of Reason," the works of Harriet Martineau, some of those of John Stuart Mill, the "Decline and Fall of the Roman Empire," some of Fourier, and many others calculated to scatter to the winds all of his former convictions.

His reading, coupled with his memory, made his company entertaining and his conversation elegant and correct. His person being agreeable, his disposition genial, and his remarks often wise and witty, it was only a little while before he became a greater favorite with Mrs. Bowers than he had ever been with her husband. She soon ingratiated herself completely into his confidence; noticed him in such a patronizing way that he very quickly told the story of his life, and with it, his great love for Phœbe Strong.

CHAPTER XXXI.

ABOUT the first thing Robbie did was to write Phœbe a long letter all about it. This letter he had from day to day delayed sending, and finally showed it to Mrs. Bowers in order that she might point out any mistakes or grammatical errors. It was a letter breathing love and hope—the letter of an ambitious boy to his first love, his idol. It was full of promise, and warm with those tender sentiments that spring from the heart. Mrs. Bowers pronounced it perfect, and advanced the opinion that, if she was a girl, she would be very proud to receive such a message from her sweetheart. The letter was given to her to mail. It never reached its destination.

One day a week or so after his advent, a letter addressed to Robert Porter was left at the Bowers' home. A few moments after its arrival it was blazing on the hearth in Judge Bowers' library.

It pains me, reader, to write that the only pious character in my novel is the most base one. That a woman of the social and religious standing of Josephine Bowers should come between an unsophisticated country boy and his rural love may seem to the reader as unreasonable. There is only one hypothesis on which to base the cause.

Josephine Bowers, for the first time in her life, was in love. She knew it, and was at first ashamed of it, and, to do her justice, I will say she laughed at the idea, drove it from her mind, banished it, buried it, strangled it, denied it with her tongue, stamped on it with her foot, but just as sure as Robbie Porter came into her presence it came back stronger than ever, and each day required a greater struggle than the preceding one. At the end of a week she was vanquished, and love—yes—and something worse, jealousy, also had just as surely taken possession of her heart and conscience as the devil takes the soul and body of his victims. In contests of this kind I have noticed that love generally wins.

She therefore began to dream, to hope, that something might happen. Then could not this boy love her as he loved Phœbe Strong. Why not? She was young; she would be rich. The judge was nearly seventy now. He was a trifle delicate, too. He could not live many years longer, and then—then; well, though she had never practiced the art of love, she was confident she could teach a few of its principles to this handsome young Virginian.

In the meantime he might marry Phœbe. She fairly shuddered at the thought. She would prevent it!

She did not at first know how, but opportunity, fate, the devil, or something aided her. She already knew Robbie's proud and sensitive nature. If he received no replies to his letters, she was sure that his independent spirit would never beg any woman's love, even though it broke his heart to lose it. She had it. She would destroy any letters that came to the house post-marked "Virginia."

Therefore on the arrival of the first one, which she felt sure was from Phœbe, and which, jealous as she was, she dared not open, she tossed into the grate, and watched it crumble to ashes, and disappear up the chimney. The letter Robbie gave her to post she care-fully locked in a drawer, fully believing that some day she would hand it to him and hear him bless her for not sending it.

Now, while it is true that Robbie had imparted to this woman most of the secrets of his heart, because he trusted her, and thought her good and true and womanly, the tender scene in the attic with his be-loved Phœbe had necessarily been omitted. It was not, therefore, with as much surprise as Mrs. Bowers expected he lamented the absence of letters.

To tell the truth, reader, Robbie had his own misgiv-ings about that very scene. His heart troubled him mightily. He was fully aware of the delicacy of the character of Phœbe, and was very much afraid that her awakening would be accompanied with a revulsion of feelings. He longed for a letter, but had sad mis-givings as to its contents. He wished, and hoped, and feared, and doubted. Then, too, Phœbe may have con-fessed all to her parents, and what must they have thought of him. He deplored the situation, and was tormented with uncertainty. But when three weeks had slipped away, and no word had come, he made up

his mind that either Phœbe hated him, or Uncle
Phineas had learned the truth and forbade her to write.
Three of her letters had already come to the house, and
all had been consigned to the flames by Josephine
Bowers. He decided, however, to write one more letter, and if that brought no reply, just as soon as he
completed his contract, to go back to Virginia, face
the consequences, and if Uncle Phineas refused him
Phœbe, persuade her to run away with him. He knew
he would win the five thousand dollars, and that would
help him and his beloved to a start in life. Filled with
these honorable thoughts and purposes he sat down in
the library, after returning from school and wrote:

"DEAREST PHŒBE AND ONLY LOVE: Why art thou
silent? Has thy Robert no longer any place in thy
heart? Has thy mind banished the memory of his face,
and has thy tongue ceased to repeat his name? Dost
know that thy silence makes heavy his heart, and is
tumbling his castles in ruins? Dost know that without thy love his hopes will perish, and his ambition
will die? If I have wronged thee, Phœbe, recall the
past and forgive me; think of the future and receive
me. Let me not say that I have builded my faith on
sand; have confessed my love to air. Help me to ful-
fill the dreams of my youth, to complete the plans of
my life; and write, write one line, one word of affection to him who yet remembers the sweetness of thy
breath; who yet recalls the beauty of thy wondrous
eyes.   ROBBIE."

"There," said Robbie, "if she does not answer that,

by Heaven! I'll lock up her image in my heart, throw away the key, and forget that I ever heard her name."

He had completed the folding, and had put the superscription upon the envelope, when somebody leaned over his shoulders and in a merry tone said:

"Writing to your girl again, I warrant! She can't think much of you not to answer your letters!"

It was Mrs. Bowers.

Her observation appeared true, and Robbie colored. She was dressed for a walk. As she already knew to whom the letter was addressed, Robbie inquired if she was going as far as the post office. She was not going that far, but if he wanted his letter mailed, she would gladly walk a block or two farther, "Just to help along a love match," she said, smiling. Robbie handed her the letter. This one she opened and read, and laid it by the side of the others.

Robbie waited hopefully, expectantly, for two weeks. No reply came. He plunged deeper than ever into his books. He said, "I will forget her!" But at night he saw her face in the stars, and in the morning he heard her voice calling "Robbie, Rob-b-i-e!" and awoke to find himself in his gilded room, in a house where at least the hearts of two people were daily longing for what they were never to possess.

CHAPTER XXXII.

NEW scenes, new situations, new faces, the fascination of study, the ultimate hope of success, kept Robbie from despair. Indeed, he was nearly happy. He could not bring his mind to believe that Phœbe had forgotten him. He still felicitated his heart with the belief that she loved him, and that she would again fall fondly into his arms the moment he appeared before her. His own affection, he was sure, was fixed.

True, he could smile, and sing, and be gay, but he never forgot. In the quiet of his chamber, in the company of his own thoughts, Phœbe's face came to him, and a vision of the old home, the terraced lawn, and the rolling river passed before his eyes. But the winter went; and, almost before he was aware, summer, soft, sensuous summer, with its green robes and violet valleys, was breathing its soft and scented airs upon Conestoga's lofty hills and verdant meadows. And as winter had thrown away her rough, uninviting costume, so had Robbie Porter discarded his plain and country-like garb.

Under the influences of that wondrous library, under the direction of Josephine Bowers, who had now become kind, solicitous and companionable; under the gentle and refined associations of a man like Judge

Bowers, my hero had again metamorphosed into another being. Study had somewhat paled his cheek, but taste had greatly improved his costume. He had grown fastidious. He wore immaculate shirt fronts, snow-like collars, gay, parti-colored ties, neat, low-cut patent leather shoes, white or embroidered vests, and sometimes duck trousers, a jaunty straw hat, and, yes, —carried a cane, when he walked out.

Why, the boy had become a dude, a bud of fashion, a patron of art in clothes, a judge of books, and a local authority on all subjects, scientific, theological, political, horse racing, law, philosophy, statuary, painting, fiction, medicine, poetry, or most anything you wanted information about. Even Judge Bowers, whose range of reading had been wide, confessed that he now got all of his current information from Robbie Porter. He had, indeed, changed. He had become a philosopher. He saw no sorrow, no grief, in any imaginary or real calamity.

He had arrived in a few short months to a mental condition many others have reached. He was ready to confess that he knew nothing. Ready to doubt anything or all things. He suspected all religions, and believed in none. He kept his promise to the judge and read the Bible from cover to cover. He found in it things most ministers missed. He threw it aside, and said man could get along without it. He never looked at it again for twenty years. He believed that death ended all; that man had no soul, that hell was a myth, heaven an imaginary place, and immortality either the dream of the fearful or the hope of the affectionate. He openly praised Fourierism, and lauded Voltaire as the matchless wit of a wondering world. Ingersoll had not yet flashed across the intellectual horizon. He knew that he was groping in darkness, yet felt as though the scales had fallen from his eyes. In his heart he thanked Judge Bowers and regarded himself under a debt of gratitude, he had no method or means of repaying. One thing he resolved, never to do anything to forfeit the good opinion this noble old man entertained of him.

The summer went fast, and the time when Judge Bowers had selected to test the speed of Dewy Iris was fast approaching.

At this time the interest in trotting horses had become greatly increased. The National Trotting Association had been organized, and all over the country it had now become the custom for local agricultural county or fair associations to offer purses for the best trotters. To induce good performances, and increase attendance, these purses were often quite large, in some instances amounting to several thousand dollars. Interest in trotting events was at its height. Flora Temple, whose record of 2:19¾, made ten years before, and which had stood the unapproachable wonder of the trotting world, was in 1867 outdone by the noble Dexter, who had spoiled the predictions of the turf prophets by lowering the record to 2:17¼. To beat, or even equal Flora Temple, was, however, the dream of hundreds of horse owners, and she was the idol of the turf.

The Lancaster County Fair was advertised in 1870 to open Thursday, August 4th. The principal feature of entertainment, the management promised, was the trotting races. Large purses were offered, and competitors flocked from miles around. There were to be three, perhaps four races each day, and the swiftest horses known to the turf world were promised to be present. For Friday, the 5th of August, the second day, there was to be a race, advertised as the 2:20 class, in which a purse of one thousand dollars was offered, six hundred dollars to the winner, three hundred dollars to the second horse, and one hundred dollars to the third, and one thousand dollars additional to the horse that would lower Dexter's record of 2:17¼, no matter if only one heat was trotted. This last purse was guaranteed by the bankers and manufacturers of Lancaster.

Seventeen horses were registered and posted as entered for this contest. Among them on the billboards appeared the name of Dewy Iris, four-year-old filly, property of S. P. Bowers, driven by Robbie Porter.

For ten years now Judge Bowers had owned the fastest horses on the Lancaster track. If there was a world-beater in that county it was generally understood that Bowers would show up with it at the race track during fair week. He had been a purse-winner for years, and with his race-track winnings had purchased Bibles and presented them to his constituents, so that there was not a woman or a voter in all Lancaster County but owned a Bible presented by their affectionate friend, S. P. Bowers.

Neither the judge nor Robbie had made known their intentions as to Dewy Iris, and Robbie had been particular never to trot her in the presence of many people. It was the judge's dream to spring a wonder, not only upon Lancaster, but upon the world. Some persons, however, had seen Robbie drive the mare a few mornings on the track before the fair opened, and secretly made up their minds that if they could get a bet the day of the race they would back Bowers' filly against the field though the great Dexter himself were present and had been allowed to enter this race.

Owing to the special purse offered in order that all entries might have a chance therefor, the distance flag was waived and the horse making a record lower than Dexter would win the special purse of one thousand dollars. The best three heats in five would win first money.

CHAPTER XXXIII.

The 5th of August was the hottest day in Lancaster, in the year of 1870. It was, too, the most exciting. I suppose there are many now living who remember a few of the stirring scenes of that day. I suppose hundreds of people can recall the melancholy fate of poor Judge Bowers. In the minds of many the memory of the vast crowds that filled the fair grounds on that day no doubt still lingers. And such a crowd, I suspect, has never congregated there since. The farmers came from the surrounding country for a distance of forty miles. They poured in from the adjacent villages. Business men closed their stores; furnaces smoldered in the iron mills; the spindle and the loom were silent; the banks shut their doors; the judges and lawyers laid aside their briefs; flags floated gayly from the tall tower of the jail, and streamers decorated the public buildings. Bands played, and bunting waved. By two o'clock, the time for the first race, ten thousand people were within the gates of the Lancaster Fair Grounds. The grand stand was crowded with fashion and with beauty. Every eye was bright with excitement, and every face was animated with joy.

"Judge Bowers," said Robbie, on the morning of this day, as he mounted his sulky to drive Dewy Iris to the

scene of the coming contest, "I have, as you know,
never driven a race, but I am going to drive this mare
to-day faster than you have ever seen a horse trot, and
faster, perhaps, than you will ever see one again.
When the sun goes down to-night, everybody will
know where Lancaster is. Dexter will be forgotten, and
Dewy Iris will be the queen of the trotting turf, and
will wear Flora Temple's crown. When the judges
announce the time after the first heat, will you kindly
hand me, in currency, the five thousand dollars?"

"I will go by the bank, and draw the money," said
the judge.

"Thanks, judge, you are a man of your word; the
soul of honor. It is not that I doubted you, but when
I have trotted one heat my contract is complete. Win
or lose, I shall immediately turn the mare over to you,
and never again, for money, for love, for fame, will I
race another horse. I will quit the scene, and start to-
night for Virginia. I will win! so have the money, as
I am fully persuaded to leave to-night."

For days this had been Robbie's dream, and he was
so impatient to depart that he could scarcely wait the
conclusion of his agreement. Of the three hundred
dollars he had now remaining about sufficient to take
him to Fredericksburg. He made up his mind to see
Phœbe, whether he won or lost.

CHAPTER XXXIV.

FATE decreed he was never to see that sweet face again. Fate, for many, many weary years thereafter detained him from Virginia. He was to see many States and pass through many experiences before he again beheld the hills and rivers of the Old Dominion.

Nevertheless, he drove gayly under the wire in front of the judge's stand, and carefully heeded the instructions for driving in a race.

Of the seventeen horses entered, only seven appeared to score. The rest were "scratched." Of these seven, four had records as low as 2:26; one had a record of 2:24, and one 2:22. The latter was the property of a Philadelphia gentleman, a bay mare, known as Get There, only six years old, traced to Abdallah, whose ancestry was founded in Imported Messenger. For this mare the owner had refused ten thousand dollars. Dewy Iris had no record, no breeding, and her looks betrayed the facts.

Her heavy head suggested the old Melbourne stock, while her ears reminded you of the old-fashioned Cap. Clays. Her long, lean barrel, with its blue and white hair, suggested a strain from Doyle's famous Blue Bull, while her lengthy, muscular arms, broad, flat knees, and well-developed chest, indicated to some that Rysdyk's

Hambletonian blood stirred in her veins. Dewy Iris was sixteen hands and better high, and her beautiful action when she moved suggested perfect harmony of points, and a correct fitting of all her joints. It was, however, in her full eyes, in her broad, flat forehead, in her moderate neck, wide, muscular, yet light, the large, dilating nostrils, the fine muzzle, the clean throat, the spacious, loosely attached windpipe, the long, deep body, and the high-set tail, that the connoisseur of the turf saw the coming winner of the day.

"Hurrah for Robbie Porter!" shouted a schoolmate, as our hero drove by. Many who heard it laughed.

A man who had seen the mare go the morning before said, "There goes a world beater." Those who heard it laughed also; some quite loud.

A few who thought they saw in this unknown nondescript the future race horse of the world went quietly to the booths and bet all they had that she would win the first heat.

Judge Bowers had already wagered one thousand dollars, even money, that Dewy Iris would not only win the first heat, but would win it in less than 2:18.

Bowers was long known to be eccentric. Many now declared him crazy. Several, however, put up money on this proposition, and went laughing around the grounds telling everybody that there was "easy money" in old Bowers to-day.

Before many wagers of this kind had been made, somebody shouted, "They're off!"

Sure enough, the word "Go," had been given, and

Judge Bowers fairly flew toward the judge's stand. His heart almost stopped beating when he saw Get there in the lead at the pole, and Dewy Iris off last, and three lengths in the rear. But as she sailed under the wire he saw Robbie Porter's pale face and compressed lips. He heard him say, coolly, easily, almost gently: "Dewy Iris, they're giving you dust. You don't take that, do you, old girl?"

Oh, how beautifully she responded to that old-time appeal! How often on the red roads of Virginia had Robbie spoken those words to her. How clearly she understood their import. She knew—she knew that Robbie wanted her to go. She knew that she was in a race; she knew that some big bay horses, a bay mare, and a couple of little chestnut fillies were spluttering down the track ahead of her. She laid her ears back, stretched out those long yellow legs, unloosed a few links, heretofore concealed in her joints, and was off— off as no other animal was ever seen to go. With never a skip, never a hop, not the slightest indication of a break, her legs working as regularly and as rapidly as the piston rods of an engine, her wide nostrils dilated, and the foam flying in feathery flakes from her lips, she literally flew away.

At the last quarter she was at the neck of Get There, and at the first half—that is, going under the wire the first time, it being a half mile oval track—she was two lengths ahead, and going like the wind.

"They're after you!" shouted Robbie, so Judge Bowers, now as near dead with delight as he had a moment before been with fear, could hear, and the mare, covered with lather, and shooting clouds of steam from her expanded ebony nostrils, seemed to let out another link. There was no overhauling her. A locomotive could not have passed her. She was trotting the race of her life; she was lowering the world's record; she was winning a fortune for Robbie Porter; she was helping Phœbe Strong. She seemed to know it all. She came tearing down the stretch, the most perfect trotting picture that ever pulled a wheel.

Where was Get There? Where were the big bays, and where were the chestnut fillies? Lost in a cloud of dust, distanced, almost forgotten by the cheering crowd, which had kept its eyes fastened on Dewy Iris from the time her driver had so beautifully taken the pole from Get There.

She passed under the wire, a clean winner by nearly the sixteenth of a mile. Get There was second, and a big bay, known as Fast Asleep, came in third.

It was some time before Robbie could induce Dewy Iris to stop, not daring to try until he passed the wire. He did not know how fast she was trotting, but he knew that Get There trotted the fastest heat of her life; and judging that she got in in 2:22 (which she did), he concluded that he had beat her by five seconds at least. His heart, however, nearly stood still till he heard the time-keeper announce, "Dewy Iris wins this heat, time 2:14½; Get—" The words were lost in the mighty shout that went up from nearly five thousand throats.

The band struck up "Brush Away that Blue-Tail

"DEWY IRIS WINS THIS HEAT—TIME 2:14½."

Fly!'' and the old darky, who was sponging the foam
and dust from Dewy Iris' mouth, broke out, keeping
time to the refrain of the spirited music:

> " Oh, Judge Bowers drove out one afternoon,
>   The people followed in coupé and 'broom,'
>   De Judge's driver was just a trifle shy,
>   But he win all de money wid a Blue-Tail Fly,
>   Oh, brush away, etc! "

And in his delight rolled over in the dust.   The air
was full of flying hats and waving handkerchiefs.

Robbie, in his sulky, waiting for the announcement,
every nerve strained and every muscle stiff, relaxed his
rigid hands and legs and literally rolled off the vehicle.
In an instant his arms were around the steaming neck
of Dewy Iris.   He pressed her long head into his big
bosom and kissed her over and over again.   He tried
to restrain his tears, but they rolled down his cheeks
like summer rain.

"Oh, Dewy Iris! Dewy Iris!" he faintly uttered, between his sobs, "I saved your life; now you have saved
mine.   You have paid me back, old girl!"

In that moment, when the happiness of his heart was
streaming from his eyes, he had a vision of the white
walls of River View; he heard the rippling Rappahannock, and breathed again the pine fragrance as it floated
on gentle zephyrs from the tall trees that gracefully
nodded on the verdant banks of that beautiful river;
again he held his blushing Phœbe in his arms, tasted
the moisture of those lovely lips, and felt her heart beat

wildly against his own; he was already miles away; but the tumultous clamor, the babbling tongues, and a consciousness that Judge Bowers was clinging to him like a vine, drove the delicious reverie away, and blotted out his picture of passion and of joy.

"Robbie! Robbie!" called the judge, looking up into that bright, but tear-stained face; "Robbie, bear up, boy. No time for tears; shout, man; laugh, shout, dance. Don't you know you have the world at your feet? Don't you know you are a greater driver than Splann? Why, man, you've 'smashed' all the records, you've paralzyed the world—you've——"

"Ten thousand dollars for your filly! old man," called a tall gentleman, as he sprang through the crowd around the horse, and shook a roll of bills under the nose of Judge Bowers.

"And you, young man, five thousand a year for you as long as the mare lives.

"Twenty thousand dollars," fairly yelled a little man, as he ducked his way to the side of Robbie, "and ten thousand for you! Money down in two hours. Is it a bargain?"

"Not for me!" said Robbie emphatically.

"Not for sale!" said the judge.

"Make way there," he cried, as he and Robbie, the aforesaid sponge holder, followed by the two gentlemen, led Dewy Iris toward the paddock.

Another wild cheer went up as they passed the grand stand.

Mrs. Josephine Bowers frantically waved her sunshade, while the band broke out with, "See the Conquering Hero Comes!"

"Judge," said Robbie, when they were out of hearing of the hubbub, "have I kept my contract?"

"You have!"

"Have you brought the money?"

"There it is!" And he handed Robbie a package of greenbacks, the mark "five thousand dollars" on a white paper band which held the bills together, just as it was when the judge drew it from the bank.

"Then the mare is yours, and good-by."

"Good-by?" stammered the judge, his eyes nearly starting from his head. "Why, what do you mean? You're certainly going to drive the race out?"

"Not for gold and precious stones!"

"I am pained, sir; I am astonished! Why, sir, you desert me in the midst of battle; you leave me on the threshold of glory. No one can drive the mare! Oh, don't, don't, Robert; if you love me, if you have gratitude and friendship, finish this race. It will ruin me if you leave me, the crowd will jeer me. Come, Robbie, you shall have the extra purse, the one thousand dollars, and first money; come, for the sake of friendship!"

The appeal was pitiful. The judge was pale and trembling, and appeared to be on the verge of collapse.

"For friendship!" said Robbie, "I will drive another heat. No more! Sell the mare as soon as the heat is concluded. You know she is treacherous, willful and uncertain. I doubt if she will trot the third heat.

She is nervous now, and only very gentle handling will soothe her, or get her to move."

"Take a whip," said the judge, handing him a short stock.

Robbie took it, bent it double, and threw it over the stable roof.

The gong was now sounding for the second heat.

The twenty minutes allowed had elapsed.

Mounting his sulky Robbie, even paler than before, drove under the wire and gayly Dewy Iris moved down to the scoring point. A loud cheer greeted horse and man.

As usual, a few of the horses were tardy, and before the first score, Judge Bowers, now having recovered his composure, stepped up to Robbie's sulky wheel and whispered: "Drive her this time, Robbie! Let the jays see what she can do. Shove her along, boy! and my will shall be made in your favor to-morrow!"

Under the rules, Dewy Iris was entitled to the pole,— that is, to a line three feet from the inside rail that encircled the course. The mare, however, was already chafing her bit, and highly nervous, so, in the scoring, Robbie did not try for the pole, but lagged a little, and took the outside, preferring not to risk the rather perilous position the pole horse is sometimes crowded into by the treachery of unscrupulous drivers. He knew that his horse was a favorite with everybody but the rival jockeys, and knew that nothing would please them better than to have a "mix up." He therefore told the starter to give the word "Go," when the other

six were right, and not to mind him.   This was agreeable, and thus handicapped, voluntarily, of course,
Dewy Iris began her scoring for the second heat.

Fortunately a few trials only were necessary, and the
"Go!" sounded loud and clear, the horses all bunched
except Dewy Iris, whose head was just over the outside
wheel of one of the chestnut fillies.

Up went a cloud of dust, blinding horse and driver,
but to the gentle word of Robbie, with his ear almost
touching the right flank of his horse—"They're giving
you dust, Dewy Iris," she bounded as a frightened deer.
In an instant, like a flash, the cloud of dust was behind;
she was flying away like a bird, as swift, as noiseless,
as beautiful.

The crowd watched her spellbound.   She went under
the wire the first time in 1:06, and as she did so Robbie
said again, gently—sweetly almost—several heard him,
"They're after you, Dewy Iris!"

She never faltered, never skipped, never shook her
head, but like an irresistible, perfect piece of mechanism
she sailed on; and went under the wire a clear winner
by nearly an eighth of a mile.

Fast Asleep was later, and Get There thirteen seconds
behind.

Dewy Iris had trotted a mile in two minutes and
twelve seconds!

CHAPTER XXXVII.

THE greeting this announcement received beggars accurate description. Men grew hoarse with shouting; women applauded till their gloves burst; the band played with a vigor that threatened to split the horns and crack the drums. Robbie Porter was literally lifted from his sulky, and on the shoulders of four strong men paraded before the grand stand. Pandemonium reigned. Dewy Iris was indeed the wonder of the trotting world. Every wire leading out of Lancaster was "hot" with the startling achievement. Judge Bowers, wild with delight, capered around the mare like a schoolboy, and when Robbie appeared to lead her to the paddock, kissed and hugged him with the enthusiasm of genuine affection.

"Come, Bowers," said the little man, who had "ducked" his way a second time to Robbie's side. "Come, Bowers, sell me your mare. Be reasonable, I'll make it twenty-five thousand dollars!"

"Nonsense!" laughed the judge, following the mare and her driver. "Why, man, you haven't seen her trot yet. I tell you, sir, there's more speed in her than that!"

"Will you take thirty thousand dollars? Money in hand as soon as the bank opens—five thousand down to bind the bargain? Is it a go?"

The little man was in dead earnest, and held in his hand a large roll of bills.

"Wait a minute!" said the judge.

"Oh, Robbie," he called, "shall I sell her? I am offered thirty thousand dollars!"

"Sell her," whispered Robbie. "I know she won't trot another heat!"

"It's a bargain!" said the judge, turning to the little man.

"There's your money! five thousand; you know me, Joe Quirrell, of Norristown. Step in here and I'll give you a draft on the First National Bank for the balance. Is that satisfactory?"

"Perfectly, sir. I know you for a man of honor."

The sale was immediately concluded.

"The mare's mine!" said Quirrell.

"The mare's yours!" replied the judge.

"Then you have no further use for me, so I'll go!" said Robbie.

"Go!" exclaimed Quirrell, his tone full of surprise. "Why, man, you're certainly hired to drive this race out? How's this, judge? Surely you don't expect me to get a driver at this late hour? Why, my God, there goes the gong for the third heat!"

"Mr. Porter," said the judge, "is under no contract with me. He was to drive her one heat. He drove the second as a favor to me. I promised him the special money and the regular purse. And, Robbie, here's your special money now!" With that he handed him a thousand-dollar bill.

"But, sir, I will pay you handsomely!" said Quirrell appealingly. "Name your price, young man, and you can have it right now!"

The gong was sounding again.

"I refuse," said Robbie quietly.

"Oh, come now! Don't treat a man that way. Name your terms. I'll hire you by the year. Give you ten thousand a year to drive for me."

"I am not a jockey, sir," Robbie answered haughtily.

"Maybe not," said Quirrell, "but you are the finest I ever saw. So, just name your price to drive this race out."

"I can't do it, I don't want to do it. All the money in Pennsylvania, sir, could not hire me!" Thus delivering himself, Robbie started to leave.

"Why, Christ Almighty!" said Quirrell, now thoroughly angry, "this looks like a job. Bowers, you've put up some game on me! Is there anything the matter with the mare? You know, as an old horseman, that such business as this doesn't go on the turf. I demand to know what this means; why this man can't drive this race out as the rules provide? Judge Bowers you're too old a man to play tricks on your friends!"

"Sir," said the judge, "you insult me! Take back your money. I don't have to sell the mare. Here—" and he stuck Quirrell's money under his nose.

"That's all right, Bowers; a bargain's a bargain with me. But if there is a trick in this, you'll spring no more trotting wonders in this community. We'll get you out of the association all right!"

This last remark touched the judge.

Quirrell was rich and powerful. The intimation that he might prefer some charges, and rule him off the turf was a little too much for the old man.

For twenty years he had been the most prominent patron of the turf in all that country. His reputation was the highest; his word was taken on every track for any amount. He was proud of his standing. To have even a shadow on it, at this time, the closing years of his life, was what touched him to the quick, pained him.

Robbie read his face, and anticipated his words. The judge was angry, and when he spoke he looked Quirrell full in the face.

"Joe Quirrell, you touch my honor now! I am too old to thrash you. I am too old and too sensitive to have my name coupled with the suggestion of tricks and frauds; but, by God, sir, I am not too old to drive a horse! I'll drive the mare myself, and then you shall apologize to me for this day's talk! Here, Pompey, bring up that mare, quick!"

The judge had divested himself of his coat, vest, collar and tie, and as the negro led up the horse, sprang into the sulky seat with the agility of a boy.

"Oh, no, judge," said Robbie, moving up, and taking the old man kindly but firmly in his arms, "I can't allow that. You might get killed. We can't afford to lose you. If it is to protect your honor, I'll drive the mare."

He lifted the old man to the ground, and quickly

vaulted into the vacated seat. Gathering up the reins, he said, "I do this for you, Judge Bowers; not for you, Mr. Quirrell."

"All right," shouted Quirrell, whose good humor had now returned. "Knock another second off the last heat, and I've another thousand dollars for you."

"Judge Bowers," he continued, turning to the old gentleman, "there's my hand. Forgive me, sir, I meant no offense."

"Well," said the judge, "since no harm's done, here's mine, and let bygones be bygones. But, I tell you, Quirrell, get that boy of mine to work for you if you can. He is perfect master of the mare, fairly loves her, and she will trot her gizzards out for him. He raised her, and she knows his voice. It will pay you, if you are going to trot her, to give him an interest in her."

"I'll do it," said Quirrell, "just as soon as he comes out of the heat. By gosh, they're off! There they go!" he shouted, as the seven horses, Dewy Iris inside and already a length ahead, shot past in a cloud of dust.

"What a goer!" exclaimed Quirrell, his eyes fixed on Dewy Iris making the first turn.

"Wonderful! Wonderful!" said Judge Bowers, shading his eyes as the mare came down the stretch, and watching her superb action with the fond gaze of genuine love.

"A thousand dollars, even money, that she does this heat in 2:10!" he continued, producing a roll of bills.

"Not on me," replied Quirrell, as the mare went under the wire like a whirlwind.

"One four and a half," yelled the time keeper to the spellbound crowd; and as the other horses came teeming along the wild cheers were turned to jeers and laughter.   Such expressions as "Push on the lines!" "Grease your buggy wheels!"   "Where'd you get that pelter?"   "Hurry up home or you'll get wet!" were shouted at the other contestants as they pounded one after another past the Judge's stand.

Dewy Iris, still going beautifully, had just swung into the stretch, fully twelve seconds ahead of Fast Asleep who, hugging the pole, closely pursued by Get There, was really doing a 2:20 clip, and as steady as a ship, when lo, Dewy Iris, making a sudden spring to one side, reared on end, on her hind legs, and pawed the dust-filled air for a second; then deliberately stopped and sat plump down between the sulky thills in the middle of the track.

All was over.

On came Fast Asleep, on came Get There.   Their respective drivers, swearing and whipping, half-blinded with dust and sweat, not prepared for the sudden obstruction that barred their way to victory, intent only on winning, could not, had they even seen Robbie's predicament, turn their horses in time to avoid a collision.

It was inevitable.   The big bay horse, his steel shoes shining in the sun, reared, and fell over the stooping shoulders of Robbie Porter, and right behind came the other horse (whose driver, seeing the situation, threw away his lines, and rolled out backward), rearing and plunging amid a wreck of broken seats, flying spokes and scraps of harness.

A wild cry, a cry of horror went up from that mighty crowd.

Strong men, men who had faced death in all its angry forms, with bloodless cheeks turned away their faces. Women screamed, wrung their hands, and fainted.

It did not seem that out of that inextricable mass of fallen horses and broken sulkies, anything could escape; but, quick as a flash, the treacherous favorite sprang away like an arrow from its bow, and, with jump after jump, her eyes bulging out till they threatened to fall from their sockets, her wide nostrils distended till it seemed her head would fall apart, dashed past the grand stand, still fastened to the sulky, with Robbie Porter hanging by one leg, his hat off, his face white as death, dangling and bouncing from behind, his head hitting the hard earth with every jump of the mare.

"Great God!" said a man, dashing toward the track, now already filled with shouting, helpless people.

"Merciful fathers!" said an old woman, with a black bonnet and white hair.

"Save him! Save him! Somebody save him!" screamed Josephine Bowers, as she fell in a dead faint and rolled to the bottom of the seats of the grand stand.

But on went the mare. There was no man hardy or brave enough to attempt to stop that irresistible force. It would have been instant death. It looked as

SHE WAS COMING UP THE STRETCH, RUNNING LIKE MAD.

though the splendid achievements of Dewy Iris were to conclude with an awful tragedy.

The driver of Get There, his ribs broken, was being carried from the field. The track was crowded thick with men, some following the mad career of the flying runaway, others trying to intercept her at various points along the course.

She was coming up the stretch again, running like mad, dragging her helpless driver behind, when, suddenly, from somewhere, nobody seemed to know, a man, taller than any other on the ground, wearing a broad-brimmed, brown straw hat, long white hair, waving out behind, a William Penn coat, the tails of which stood straight out, working his long arms like those of a windmill, made his way through the staring, awe-struck mob of men.

His hat flew off, but with long strides he ran straight for Dewy Iris.

It did not seem that anybody in their right senses would attempt to stop the mare, but of a certainty this was the purpose of the old man.

As she came nearer, he stopped right in her path; threw up both arms, and shouted so that he could have been heard a quarter of a mile.

"Whoa, Dewy Iris!"

For an instant it seemed the wild animal paused, but only an instant, but in that instant those powerful long arms shot out and caught in their muscular hands the iron bit of the mare. The concussion, the shock, was terrible. Only a Hercules could have stood up after contact with such a force. Only muscles of steel could have stayed that almost irresistible advance. As it was, Dewy Iris was forced back on her haunches and thence over on her side, so that horse and man rolled in the dust together.

"Bravo! Bravo!" shouted ten hundred voices.

"Hurrah for the Quaker!" yelled a thousand men.

"Three cheers for the broad brim!" shouted others.

Quick as lightning the old man was on his feet.

"Hold her," he said, as the crowd pressed around.

A dozen fell upon the prostrate animal, and in another minute Robbie Porter, in the old man's arms, his hair matted with blood and dust, all vestige of life apparently fled from his being, blood pouring from his mouth and nose, was being tenderly carried from the scene.

The old man, the rescuer, was Phineas Strong.

CHAPTER XXXVIII.

THE reader, I know, will pardon me if I take him from the tumultuous scenes of the racetrack to the green fields of Virginia.

It is really nowadays but a short distance, and my purpose is to again gaze upon the charming Phœbe, whom, as you no doubt remember, we left sound asleep in Robbie Porter's bed, that dreary morning in November, less than a year ago.

It is long ago conceded that great grief induces sound, and sometimes long sleep. We have all of us been told that the Savior of the world slept in the Garden of Gethsemane, though in the shadow of death itself. It is not, therefore, surprising that Phœbe, whose heart had all the preceding day been very heavy and very sad at the prospect of Robbie's departure, would, when once overcome by the drowsy god, long continue a victim of his charms. She did not, therefore, appear at the breakfast table, and did not wake until the day was already far advanced.

At last, however, her eyes opened, and her gaze fell upon the placid face of Rachel Strong, who at that very moment was bending over her.

Just what were the sensations of Phœbe at thus finding herself discovered in this situation, I am not prepared to say. Her face turned white and then red; she covered it with her hands and began to cry.

"Phœbe! Phœbe," at last spoke the good woman, "surely, thee did—" she hesitated, "did not sleep here last night?"

She almost hoped Phœbe would deny what seemed all too palpable. Phœbe was a stranger to falsehood, and could no more express it with her tongue, than she could in her face. And even had she desired, there was no probable hypothesis she could advance that would explain her presence in Robbie's bed, in her night robes; she, therefore, concluded to admit what seemed uselessness to deny, and abide the consequences.

"My mother," she moaned piteously, "but I loved him so, I couldn't help it. It was my fault; besides we were married, we are married. Thee knows that the Quaker marriage is complete, lawful, when each gives himself or herself to the other. Heaven knows how sacred is ours. Oh, mother, if thee has ever loved, thee can, thee will, forgive me! Take me in thine arms, and tell me that thou lovest me still."

She threw her arms about the neck of the good woman, drew her sweet, kind face to her own, and kissed it again and again.

"Oh, Phœbe, Phœbe, thee has disgraced us! Thy father will be heart-broken, should he know it. Nothing but woe will come of it, Phœbe. It will all come back to thee in after life. 'Chickens come home to roost,' is an old saying and a true one. I fear thy father's wrath, should aught happen of it."

"Oh, mother, help me! Don't tell him! Robbie will soon come back, and then we will be married in the big front room, in the presence of thee and him, and all the servants. No harm will be done. Thee won't tell him? Promise me that thee won't?"

"I promise," said Rachel, and gave the forgiving kiss. For the present Phœbe's reputation was safe.

After receiving Robbie's first letter the old-time light of happiness illumined her beautiful face. A second letter came, telling about his new home and Dewy Iris, and Phœbe was apparently happier than ever.

She felt secure in her mother, and her faith in Robbie was fixed, unalterable. In her heart she built an altar of love, around which, in sweet fragrance and royal colorings, flourished the flowers of perpetual affection. Should they die or perish, Phœbe hoped to fade and perish with them. She had no dreams, no hopes, beyond this love. It was her world, the orbit in which she daily revolved. In it with her was Robbie Porter. This was all. All that she dreamed, all that she desired. It was her daily wish, often thought, her nightly prayer, often expressed, that the Infinite Ruler of the universe, who had given her the power to love, would give her the courage to die, should she lose this object of her rich, pure, unselfish, holy passion.

But the time came when Phœbe's days were despairing ones, and her nights even sleepless. Robbie's letters had ceased. The spring had come, and the honeysuckle blossoms were sending their fresh fragrance around the peaceful scene. The birds caroled in the trees, and the trout sparkled in the shining river. The summer came and the fullness of ripening August was seen in the rosy apples of the trees, in the golden corn of the meadows, and in the whitening oats of the hillside.

But, alas, poor Phœbe! Nature's varied beauty, nature's prodigal gifts, had no longer charms for her. The bloom was gone from her cheeks, the light had faded in her wondrous eyes, the music had deserted her voice, and the elasticity of youth was lacking in her limbs. Trustfully, day by day, she believed; faithfully, day by day, she hoped, till at last hope died in her heart and despair took possession of her mind.

It was the first day of August, in the evening, while sitting by her father's side, she suddenly burst into a fit of uncontrollable weeping. Her grief increased to such a degree, that she grew hysterical, and at last, fell swooning to the floor.

Tenderly Phineas Strong took her in his arms, and calling "Mother! mother!" carried her to her room, and, as he laid her on the bed, for the first time detected her condition. The revelation came to him so suddenly as to deprive him, for the moment, of both the power of locomotion and of speech.

"Mother," he finally gasped, pointing to the prostrate and lifeless form, "what does this mean? Does thee see? Thee must have noticed it."

"Yes, Phineas, I have noticed it. I wanted to tell thee, but she begged me day after day, hoping he would come, that I had not heart to deny her!"

"Who come?" queried Phineas.

"Robert!"

"Robert," echoed the old man; "Robert—Robert Porter. No, Rachel, thee must be mistaken! Robert is too honorable!"

"That is what she thought; that is what I thought; that is what we all thought; but she has not even heard from him since a month after he left, though she has written him repeatedly. The letters do not come back, so he must have received them."

"There is something wrong here, Rachel. Robbie Porter is not that kind of a boy; where did thee say he had gone?"

"Lancaster, Pennsylvania."

"And does thee remember with whom it was he was living?"

"Bowers, yes; a Judge Bowers. I am sure that is the name."

"Mother," said Phineas Strong earnestly, "she is safe in thy hands. Console her, comfort her. I go to find Robbie Porter. I will return with him, if he be yet in the land of the living."

"Thee will not start to-night, Phineas?"

"Yes, to-night, at once. I will mount Queen Bess and will be in Washington by early dawn; in Baltimore by sundown, and there will get a fresh mount from my friend, Hiram Holliday, the horse dealer. I ought to be home in six days with Robbie. Farewell," he said, leaning over and pressing a kiss to the upturned lips of his wife, and the old man was gone.

Ere the sun had risen he was crossing the bridge which spanned the Potomac River at Washington.

But that same sun, pouring its relentless rays upon this sacred old head, and his wearied horse, compelled both to seek shade and rest, so that it was nearly two o'clock, August 5th, when Phineas Strong rode into the city of Lancaster.

The fences, barns, and rocks, as he rode along, apprised him of the fact that the county fair was being held.

The posters that met his gaze at nearly every corner also told him that Dewy Iris, property of S. P. Bowers, driven by Robert Porter, was on that day to contest for the purses offered in the 2:20 race. He, therefore, rode on to the fair grounds, passed the gate, gave his horse to the care of a negro, and had just seated himself at the end of the grand stand nearest the paddock, intending to speak to Robbie as he came from the course. He had barely adjusted himself on the wooden seat when the collision took place.

CHAPTER XXXIX.

"A DOCTOR, call a doctor," commanded Phineas Strong, as he took the limp and lifeless Robbie to the shelter of the grand stand.

The doctor came, bent over the body, listened attentively, and announced in a professional, unfeeling way that the heart still beat.

By this time Josephine Bowers, who had now recovered her senses, arrived before the doctor and his prostrate victim.

"My carriage, quick!" she said, seeing her coachman standing near.

She knelt down in the dust, unmindful of her summer silk, and took Robbie Porter's head in her lap. Tenderly she wiped the blood from his face, and gently stirred the air with her perfumed fan.

"To my house!" she commanded, as the carriage appeared.

It was a large, richly upholstered victoria, with wide, deep cushions, and into it stepped Phineas Strong, with Robbie in his arms, as though he had been an infant.

The doctor and Mrs. Bowers followed, and the whole party proceeded by the nearest route to her home, where Robbie, still carried by Phineas Strong, still unconscious, was laid upon his own bed.

All known restoratives were applied, but in vain. His eyes opened not, his lips parted not, save to mutter guttural sounds, and emit clots of blood.

An examination showed his ankle bone was broken, a deep cut in the small of the back, evidently made by a horse's hoof, several contusions over the right ear, the skull fractured at its base just above the muscles of the neck, and considerably depressed.

After four hours of labor, and with the aid of two assistant brother physicians, the doctors agreed that the injuries were fatal, and said death would ensue within a few hours, in a day at the furthest.

"No! no!" almost screamed Mrs. Bowers, "you must not say that; you must save him. There must be some way. Oh, say there is!"

"There is none, unless," added one of the doctors, "we could perform an operation. Remove the pressure of the broken skull, animation might be restored—there is one chance in a thousand."

"Take the chance," pleaded the woman. "He is strong, he will recover. Oh, do try!"

"We are not surgeons, Mrs. Bowers," replied one of the doctors. "There is only one man in America who could undertake so delicate an operation, and he would charge a thousand dollars!"

"And who is he?" asked Phineas Strong.

"Dr. Langdon, of Philadelphia."

The name, everybody thought, rather startled the quiet Quaker, and he was seen to change color. He was about to reply, but before he could do so Josephine

Bowers broke out with: "Oh, send for him at once. Telegraph him, have him take the first train. Go, quick. I will pay ten thousand dollars! Hurry!" she continued. "Do, doctor, run!" and she bundled one of the doctors from the room. "There," handing him a twenty-dollar bill, "telegraph his expenses, tell him that he can name his own fee. Do go!" she entreated.

All night they sat by the bedside, Phineas Strong and Josephine Bowers. She learned his name and guessed the rest. And, without directly telling him so, contrived to create the impression that Robbie Porter was now affianced to one of the richest ladies in all Lancaster, who would, no doubt, be at his side the moment she was apprised of the disaster.

It was about four o'clock in the morning when Phineas Strong rose from his chair, took Robbie's hand in his own, looked lovingly and sadly into his face, turned to Mrs. Bowers and said:

"There is nothing I can do. Should Robert recover and need money, send direct to me. To my mind he is already beyond hope. My daughter is ill at home, perhaps dying. I do not care to meet the physician who is to perform the operation. Thy kindness will be rewarded. Should he die, kindly inform me. Farewell." So saying he walked from the room. Four days later he rode into his dooryard at River View.

It was dusk, no one had seen him approach. He entered his home, and walked direct to Phœbe's room.

The cry of an infant greeted his ears, as he gently pushed aside the door.

CHAPTER XL.

It was ten o'clock before the train which bore Dr. Langdon arrived in Lancaster. It was nearly noon before his examination of Robbie Porter determined him what to do. Robbie still lived, but his eyes remained closed and his tongue powerless. He was like a dead man save that he breathed. The power to move his body, raise his hands, or shift his legs was gone. Complete paralysis seemed to have taken possession of every muscle and every limb.

The excitement attending the runaway and its apparent fatal results so completely occupied the minds of the Bowers' household it was not till the next morning, the absence of the judge excited remark. In the confusion of evening, and in the grief that seemed to pervade every heart, many reasons might have been advanced why he did not appear. It was possibly thought by some that he was too deeply affected. It was generally known he had been the cause of Robbie's accident, having urged him to drive against his will. This, many argued, would so touch the judge, whose heart was so deeply sensitive, that he could not look upon his dying friend. At any rate, the judge did not appear either at the supper or the breakfast table. The noon hour came and still no judge.

Four doctors, Mrs. Bowers, and all of the servants, were occupied most of the afternoon with the patient. Opiates had to be administered, bandages made, messages sent, and errands run, so that the house was bustle and hurry and excitement till near sundown.

The operation, by which the doctors hoped to save Robbie Porter's life and return him to consciousness, consisted first, in shaving all the hair from the back part of the head; and in sawing away pieces of skull from around the fracture, and the adjusting these pieces so as to remove all pressure from the brain. The task was not only an extremely delicate one, but necessarily tedious.

That a patient reduced to such extremities should survive, there was only a remote possibility; and the anxiety induced by its performance was uppermost in the minds of every one. The adjacent neighbors, the servants, and Josephine Bowers above all, were so completely absorbed in the prospect of the untimely fate momentarily expected to overtake poor Robbie, that Judge Bowers was really overlooked, forgotten.

The sun was setting that warm Saturday when attendants at the fair grounds found him crouching in a corner of the stable that had been used by Dewy Iris.

The old man was stark naked. In front of him, torn into fragments, lay the five thousand dollars given him by Joe Quirrell. The draft for twenty-five thousand was held in his bony hands, and as the attendant who discovered him entered, he was murmuring in a plaintive tone:

"In the first chariot were red horses; and in the second chariot black horses; and in the third chariot white horses; and in the fourth chariot grizzled and bay horses.

"And I looked and beheld a pale horse, and his name that sat on him was Death."

They led him from the gloomy shadows of the stable, and the dying rays of the sun fell across his white and wrinkled face. One glance was sufficient to confirm the suspicion. From his eyes the look of reason had died out, never to return. The old man was a helpless imbecile.

The excitement of the race, the joy of its first success, and the awful catastrophe attending the conclusion, were too much for this high-strung, nervous, yet tender-hearted old man. The horrible thought that his enthusiasm and pride had caused the death of his noble *protégé*, whom he already loved as a son, was more than he could stand. His old heart broke then and there, and from that powerful throne upon which for years burned with undiminished luster the light of learning, of justice, and a warm affection, there forever fled that sweeter light of reason.

What many had for the last few years predicted as to the mental condition of Judge Bowers was now apparent.

The heartless said:

"Well, the old judge is crazy at last!"

"Just as I expected!" said another.

"Pretty near it long ago!" said a third.

Late that evening they took him to the Norristown asylum for the insane.

The Monday evening after the accident, Robbie Porter opened his eyes, and in a vague sort of way surveyed the ceiling of his own bedchamber. His glance, wandering from one familiar object to another, finally rested upon the tear-stained and now haggard face of Josephine Bowers. She was sitting by his side, and the tears were coursing over her face and falling silently into her lap.

The flush of youth had fled her cheeks, and her eyes were red and swollen.

For many minutes Robbie contemplated this picture of woe, trying vainly in some way to reconcile it to what he imagined must be the condition of things. Slowly, painfully, the vision of the terrible scene of the race-track passed before him. His head thumped and ached, and he put his hand up to stop the pain. He had no idea of the time; the room was heavily shaded, and the parting sunbeams were throwing soft shadows over the scene.

Long, however, he looked upon the weeping woman.

"Why was she here?" he thought.

"Where was the judge?" and "Who caught the runaway?" These were some of the thoughts of that poor distressed head. At last he spoke. "Was anybody else hurt?"

For an instant Mrs. Bowers doubted her ears. She never expected to hear him speak again. A look of intense astonishment, of doubt, overspread her face.

It was one of joy when she turned it and beheld his wondering gaze, full of pity, fixed upon her own.

"Oh!" She gasped it out, and clutched the bedding. "Oh!" she said again, pressing a hand over her heart. "You—you—can—can—speak?"

"Why, yes, though it is painful—b——"

"Stop!" she said quickly. "You must not talk, you must not think, you must not know, not for days. Here, close your eyes. Merciful God!" she went on, sliding to her knees by the side of the bed. "Forgive me for my doubt. Forgive me for my ingratitude. Never again, oh, never again, will I question Thy mercy and Thy goodness!"

Her sincerity was so evident it was pitiful.

"How long," asked Robbie, as she composed herself in her chair, "have I lain here?"

"Oh, don't talk, please don't!" she said appealingly, passing her hand gently over his mouth. "The doctor said you mustn't even think for days yet. Just keep quiet, and I will tell you everything. You won't talk, will you?"

"Not if you will tell me truly who stopped the runaway."

This, of all others, was the question she most dreaded, and most disliked to answer.

"An old man," she replied.

His eyes mutely but unmistakably demanded to know his name.

"Phineas Strong," she answered quietly.

She feared the effect, but there seemed no escape.

Robbie spoke not, only closed his eyes, and his help-less hands failed utterly to conceal the tears that streamed over his cheeks, and wet either side of the pillow.

"There!" she said tenderly, soothingly, "don't cry. It was the bravest deed that was ever done. Lie quiet now, till I get you some nourishment. Don't think, or speak till I come back. Then I will tell you all about it." She quitted the room a changed woman and, strange to say, with a heart fairly bounding with joy; lighter far than it was on her wedding day.

CHAPTER XLI.

THUS it was, reader, that, about the time in that old dark room at River View there was born upon the sea of life a frail, budding blossom, the mutual pledge of a sinless sin, the life of the young, strong, powerful Robbie Porter was also struggling for existence.

Fate decreed that they should some day meet, and fate decreed that these two should live. Fate decreed that face to face, bosom to bosom, father and daughter should one day be folded in each other's arms.

Phineas Strong, with tread lighter than his heart, tiptoed to the bed on which lay Phœbe and her infant daughter, now closing its fourth day's existence in a world, which, in spite of tears, in spite of broken hopes and heavy hearts, in spite of lost loves, in spite of wasted wealth, in spite of false friends, in spite of open enemies, is yet a world of beauty, of goodness and of desire.

"Phœbe!" gently spoke the old man, leaning over the prostrate form of his daughter. But Phœbe slept. The baby cried louder.

Reaching over, and lifting the bawling mite into his arms, Phineas Strong pressed the bundle of dimity and muslin against his big breast, seated himself in a low rocker, and softly hummed "Ride a cock horse to Brambury Cross," his hand and foot keeping time, when Rachel Strong entered the room.

"Phineas!" she exclaimed, going quickly to his side, and pressing a kiss upon his forehead.

The baby had ceased to cry.

"Mother!" said Phineas, taking one of her hands in his own, and drawing her to him.

"Hush!" he continued. "The baby is sleeping!" She sat down by his side, still holding one of his hands.

"And what about Robert?" she asked.

He began and told her everything in connection with his trip, and concluded his narrative with the statement: "Not caring to meet Dr. Langdon, I left the scene. Robert is now dead, as the doctor told me there was no possible chance of his recovery!"

It never occurred to Phineas Strong that Phœbe might wake and hear this part of his discourse. It had been his intention to tell her that Robbie was hurt, and might recover, and unless he received from Mrs. Bowers the announcement of his death, to go again in a few weeks and bring him home.

Phœbe, however, had really awoke before the narrative concluded, and had heard all about the accident.

Phineas Strong, therefore, had hardly finished his sentence, when a scream, loud and piercing, blood chilling, issued from the bed clothing, rang through the room, and penetrated every apartment of the old house.

The servants in the kitchen heard it, and came flying to the scene. It was a wail, a scream, whose intonations reflected the grief and agony of a breaking heart.

Phineas sprang to his feet, let go the baby, and took the distracted mother in his arms. It was with difficulty his strong grasp could restrain her impulse to pitch herself headlong from the bed.

"Phœbe! Phœbe!" he commanded, "do compose thyself. It may not be so bad! There, there, don't take on so. He may recover!"

Poor Phœbe was sobbing, and her bosom trembled as if shaken with au ague.

"Oh, father! father!" she moaned. "I dreamed it! I saw it! He is dead! Robbie! My Robbie is dead! Oh, father, let me die too! There is nothing more now. Nothing but disgrace! Nothing but death!"

Phineas gently forced her upon the pillow, and taking the baby from Rachel, who fortunately had rescued it as it slid from his hands, placed the little thing in her arms.

"There, there," he continued soothingly, "for baby's sake, thee must live. Think of the little one. It will need a mother's love, a mother's care. Look at the little thing; its blue eyes are open!"

The baby had actually opened its little eyes, and was gazing with a wondering expression, first at Phœbe's face, and then at the face of the old man.

"Oh, take it away!" begged Phœbe, "take it away. I want to die, and hope it will die with me. I could not bear to live now. To look at his child would only remind me of my dishonor; that will haunt me daily, and" (pushing the infant from her breast), "thee will be the living sign of my shame."

She buried her face in her pillow, and sobbed with unrestrained interruption. Consoling, loving words from father and mother at last lulled her to quiet, and long after midnight, to sleep.

But, in the morning, more poignantly than ever, it seemed, her grief came back, so that ere the day closed she had sobbed herself sick, and was raving in a fever of delirium. She grew rapidly worse, and a physician from Fredericksburg was sent for. He came daily for five weeks. The last day he came he brought a letter for Phineas Strong. It was postmarked "Lancaster, Pa." It was a note from Josephine Bowers. It read:

"PHINEAS STRONG.

"DEAR SIR: Pursuant to request, I write to inform you that your nephew, Robert Porter, died yesterday in a Harrisburg hospital. His clothes I have this day forwarded to your address by Adams Express Company. His injuries required surgical operations, which ended his life. Have attended to everything. All bills are paid.   Respectfully,
                    "JOSEPHINE BOWERS."

They did not show this to Phœbe. The poor girl was already beyond human aid or medical skill, and yet had that letter contained tidings of Robbie Porter's recovery; that he was alive, the prospect of seeing him again would have revived the dying girl, and I verily believe she would have lived, would have recovered, would have smiled again, would have blushed, and would have hugged to her wasted breast the tender little plant that was now drawing sustenance from a good-hearted black woman, who was robbing her own child that little Phœbe, as the baby was called, might not perish.

The doctor lingered long at River View that day, seeming loath to tell these good people that there was nothing more he could do for the broken-hearted patient. True, the fever had disappeared, and there was a faint hope of her recovery. But she refused all nourishment and had sunk into a hopeless, helpless melancholy. Neither cheery words, nor solace, nor promises of travel, nor sweet assurances of forgiveness, complete, tender and touching, not even the love of her baby, could revive her spirits, or kindle the light of yore anew in those wondrous eyes.

By her side her hands rested, transparent and thin. Her face had become a bluish white, and her once red lips pale as ashes. Her eyes had sunk down deep behind the shadows of those long lashes, and were now too dry and set and hard for even tears to flow.

The beautiful Phœbe, reader, the healthy, blushing, innocent, pure, good, tender-hearted Phœbe, was changed to a ghost-like wraith, whose marble brow and coal black hair formed almost a horrible contrast to gaze upon.

Her pulse throbbed, and her heart beat, but her tongue long ago ceased to speak. She looked at nothing, asked for nothing, and rarely heard anything. When they brought her baby, in the hope to cheer her, or arouse her from her lethargy, her face put on a painful expression; and now the little thing was never brought into her room.

On departing that day the doctor told Phineas Strong there was no use in his coming again.

"Medicine," he said, "will do her no good. Her affection is one of the heart. If you could persuade her to eat something, she might get well, but without stimulants or nourishment there is no hope." He rode away.

In vain Rachel prepared one tempting morsel after another. They were refused. In vain she coaxed, and pleaded; Phœbe ate not, smiled not, spoke not. And so the end came; so quietly, so peacefully, that those who watched her could scarcely discern when the animate ceased and the inanimate began. Around her mouth, however, just as the breath escaped, some angel painted a smile, a smile of peace, which lingered there. to light up again with the sign of life that pale sweet face.

When they laid her out, clutched in her hand, in the dying grasp of parting existence, was found the tintype picture Robbie Porter had sent her from Baltimore.

In the eyes of all who were cognizant of her melancholy story, Phœbe Strong had committed the unpardonable sin. Therefore, except from those of Phineas Strong, his wife Rachel, and those faithful black people, to whom Phœbe had always been an idol, no tears fell on her bier.

Under a huge cedar in that little burying ground, beside the grave of the color bearer, whose bravery had waved the flag of his country before the belching cannon of Fredericksburg and Chancellorsville, they laid the body of the fairest of all Virginia's fair daughters. But, reader, no long line of somber mourners, with bowed heads, gathered at her grave. In the presence of the awful shadow, Death, no consoling neighbors came to solace or to cheer. No, not one. Her pall bearers were four black men; her only white mourners were Phineas Strong and his wife. Hand in hand they left the new grave.

"Chickens come home to roost!" said Rachel.

"Chickens come home to roost!" replied Phineas.

CHAPTER XLII.

WERE this story all fiction, and made no pretense to anything but the creation of fancy, it would have been an easy matter to have spared the reader the pain which the death of so sweet a character as Phœbe no doubt causes. Fidelity to the truth of my narrative compelled a description and an account of that melancholy event. The untimely, unexpected and peculiar circumstances surrounding the death of so virtuous, so amiable a character induced no end of talk in the neighborhood. By degrees the story of the unhappy romance, and the knowledge of its living sequel became the theme of every tongue, and for years its sad incidents lingered in the memory of all.

No sympathy, however, expressed or implied, was ever extended to the unhappy Strongs. In the eyes of a censorious public, the indiscretion of poor Phœbe had met with its logical reward. In the misery of her parents, whose grief, silent, tearless, was deep and permanent, the hand and judgment of God were seen, and, I fear, applauded.

It was not very long, therefore, until those neighbors, debtors of Phineas Strong, one by one discharged the obligations they owed, and this done, shunned more and more the inhabitants of River View. Mothers and sisters, though they recalled in whispers dead Phœbe's name, promptly forgot the scene of her life and death. For the little waif whose tenacity made it an unwilling and motherless survivor, they conceived a feeling very much like horror. They described it as a nameless thing, and used the fact of its existence as an illustration to point a moral.

It was not very long, therefore, before those social barriers once erected about the good Quaker and his household, and once demolished, were again reared, higher, stronger than before. His goodness, his generosity, his frankness were all forgotten. His daughter's conduct had dishonored her name, and from the pale of respectability banished also those of Phineas and Rachel. And though it was known that Robbie Porter was the father of the child, the recreant lover, and the real cause of the death of the broken-hearted girl, not one word of blame or censure was attached to him. He was very young, and Phœbe was so much older, so near being an old maid, that she was at fault.

"It served her right!" said the widow Kemper. "And she got just what all forward girls get! So nice, too; wouldn't ever dance because the men put their arms round her. Yes, I've often heard say that they who are prudes in public, sin very easy in private. So jealous, too, she was. Why, she wouldn't even let Robbie Porter go home with the girls from parties. She was always tagging around after the lad. She never went to ride that she didn't have him with her. Well, I hope she's got enough of him. Even told my daughter once that *she* was too young to have a beau. Why, she must have been thirty, if she was a day. Well, laws knows, Dora never wanted her fellow, though I make no doubt Dora could have had him. Still he was as fine a young man as there is in these parts, and Dora might have gone further and fared worse, as the sayin' is. Ah, well, it's a warnin' to all young girls, and old ones, too, for a matter of that. They should have husbands for their beds before they have babies for their cradles—remember that!" she said, addressing the blushing Dora.

At that very moment Dora Kemper was thinking of Robbie Porter, and inwardly hoping the report of his death was false. Had he entered the home of the Kempers then, mother and daughter would have welcomed him, the former with extended hands and voice of gladness, and the latter with the most winning smile, the most modest blushes a young, ardent and designing maiden could employ.

And in this way the female portion of the neighborhood gradually consigned Phœbe's memory to oblivion, and subjected her parents and child to social ostracism. Therefore the new Phœbe, a blue-eyed, brown-haired creature, with her mother's beauty and her father's fairness, was permitted, like some undiscovered flower, to grow up in isolation, with only the companionship of her grandparents and the faithful negroes, whose loyalty never faltered and whose affection never waned.

Fate, as I before observed, decreed she should live, and in time both Phineas and Rachel took to their old hearts, with all the tenderness and solicitude the indulgent aged lavish upon the young, this nameless offspring of unconsecrated love.

In that charming scene where we first met her beautiful mother, watched by loving eyes and led with tender hands, the fairy idol of the blacks, and the sole thought of her grandparents, we will, for the present leave her, and journey again to the bedside of the hero of my tale, whom we left, two chapters back, wearily wondering, and trying to conceive the circumstances which brought Phineas Strong to Lancaster.

CHAPTER XLIII.

JOSEPHINE BOWERS returned with a tray, on which smoked a cup of fragrant tea, an egg, which diffused that delicate and peculiar flavor which only an egg, unhampered with the toil of migration, is sure to emit. There was also some brown toast, some yellow butter, and some quince jelly, which looked very much like the quince jelly Aunt Rachel and Phœbe made at River View. Pursuant to directions, in the jelly Mrs. Bowers had injected an opiate, and Robbie, who had but just awoke, as it were, no sooner completed the eating of the repast than he lapsed into a gentle, apparently a natural sleep, and his faithful nurse watched the color of life come back again to his pale face.

While it is true Robbie had not, in four days, opened his eyes, and was to all intents and purposes dead, he had not in reality slept. The nap he was now taking was, therefore, the first natural one since the accident. It was not surprising then that the effect of the opiate lasted a long while. Indeed it was near the close of the following day when he again opened his eyes.

As they soon fell upon those of Josephine Bowers, who was gazing into his face with a solicitous fondness, he was still ignorant of the lapse of time. The fact that she was there, lent probability to the thought that he just awoke from a short nap. His sensations, how-ever, were completely changed. Much of the pain from his head and back and limbs had gone; his mind was clearer, his eyes felt brighter, and he could talk with ease.

In Josephine Bowers he noticed a great change. Her former tear-stained face was now almost radiant; her gray eyes shone with a light he had never before observed—a soft glow, expressing warmth and tender-ness. Her gown, too, was different. She had changed it while he slept. It was now a rather gay-colored material, close fitting about the waist, and fastened at the neck with a gold clasp, made in the design of a heart. In its center shone a diamond. It was very pretty and very odd. Robbie had never seen it before. On a table, in a large vase, was a bouquet of fresh cut flowers, roses, leaves, and graceful grasses. The fra-grance they exhaled were wafted toward him by the motion of a fan the lady waved gently in her jeweled hand.

The soft light of the room, the perfumed gown she wore, the sweet flowers, the immaculate counterpane, his own spotless linen, the neatness, suggesting the most ardent attention to detail, produced an effect upon Robbie more delicious than he had ever known. It all seemed like a dream. Lost in the contemplation and quiet enjoyment of this scene, his reveries were continued for several moments.

"Is there anything I can do for you, Robbie?" spoke Josephine Bowers, in a voice low and sweet, bending over and pushing a stray curl back from his forehead. He had never heard her speak like that before; she never before called him "Robbie." Her voice, full of tenderness, had a charm he never before observed. Slowly he turned his eyes and said:

"Tell me everything!"

"Perhaps," she replied, "you could eat something now?"

"Why, I just ate!"

"That was yesterday."

"Yesterday?"

"Yes!"

He closed his eyes for a moment, then asked:

"How long have I lain here?"

"Four days."

"And you say Uncle Phineas was here?"

"Yes."

"Is he here now?"

"No."

"And where is the judge?"

"Now," she said, "the doctor says you must not talk. I will leave Zeb to wait on you for a few moments while I prepare you something to eat. Then, if you go to sleep, why, to-morrow, I'll tell you everything. Remember, you must not talk."

Zeb White was a black man who had been a servant to Judge Bowers for thirty years. He loved the judge, and loved Robbie Porter. He had asked to be allowed to assist in the care of the invalid. He was strong, faithful, and gentle, a natural nurse.

"Zeb!" said Robbie, extending his hand so as to grasp that of the black man, "where is Judge Bowers?"

"Now, Mister Robbie, you don' ain't to know, 'cause, you see, the judge might be all right in a day or so, so we made it up not to tell you."

"Tell me, Zeb?"

"Can't do it, sah."

"Is he hurt?"

"Can't say, sah."

"But, Zeb."

" 'Tain't no use to 'but' ; I done tole her I wouldn't tell, an' I won't."

"Where's the mare, Zeb?"

"Dunno."

"Don't know?"

"Look hy'ar, Mister Bob, you 'scuse me, but 'structions is not to let you talk.   Ef you talk, I'se got to go outer de room and set in de hall.   Rec'on I'll hab t' go."

"You need not go.   I will stop," said Robbie.

Mrs. Bowers soon appeared, and a tempting meal was placed before him.   He ate and slept again.   The next morning found him so improved that the doctor pronounced him doing nicely and predicted a rapid recovery.   By degrees he learned from Mrs. Bowers, whose attention increased rather than diminished, the whole dreadful effect of the runaway: That his friend, the judge, was hopelessly insane; that Dewy Iris had been taken home by Joe Quirrell; that nobody had been able to drive her, and that Quirrell had sent nearly

every day to inquire if Robbie would recover. Mrs.
Bowers had been appointed conservator of her husband's estate, and his own money had been deposited
in the large iron safe in the library. Of the conduct of
Phineas Strong at the race-track he had received an
elaborate account from her, and a most enthusiastic
one from Zeb. For some reason Robbie could not yet
divine, she evaded all reference to Phineas' visit
to the house, and day by day put off giving him a
detailed account of his further conduct.

Thus nearly four weeks went by, and as each day
brought health and strength to the invalid, so it seemed
to bring increased happiness to his attentive nurse.

Neither the cares her husband's condition brought,
nor the thought of it caused any sorrow to Josephine
Bowers. She grew more radiant, more gracious each
day. Everybody noticed it, and everybody remarked
it. For the first time in all her life this woman began
to anticipate happiness. In her heart was dawning the
light of a new revelation, a revelation which sooner or
later comes at least once to every human heart, and
until it does come the true functions of the human heart
are never known.

She was almost happy. She was on the very threshold of the sole purpose of life. She was soon to realize
the only true compensation life gives to those who
choose to endure its cares and disappointments. For
this new, changed condition of things, in her religious
reverence, she mentally thanked God.

In the awful tragedy of the race-track she saw His

beneficence exercised for her. In the removal of her aged husband she recognized the mercy of God, who always takes care of His own. In the sudden departure of Phineas Strong she saw His hidden and mysterious work. In the nursing of Robbie Porter she saw God's way of winning his young heart.

"For," she thought, "his gratitude will inspire him to love me, and if I can contrive in some way to keep him from Virginia, in a little while, only a little while, he will understand. God, who has brought everything about so far, will show me the way."

Thus she thought, and a way suggested itself; and in the prospect of completing this imaginary plan of Divinity for her perfect bliss, she grew happier, lighter, rosier, and more tender. By the time Robbie was able to sit up he had become very fond of his beautiful nurse. He regarded her as the most noble, most devoted woman he had ever read about. Fit, he thought, to adorn, as the heroine, the pages of any fiction.

In her eyes he saw nothing but tenderness; in her face he read no guile; and in her soft voice heard only the tones of goodness and affection. She would read to him each day, and as the shades of approaching night gathered about his couch, until the outlines of her form and face were hardly visible, linger by his bedside and talk to him of the glorious future that awaited him in his chosen profession at the bar.

CHAPTER XLIV.

NEARLY a month had elapsed since the accident, and, apparently, the only unhappy or restive person over the event was Robbie Porter. He was now able to sit up, and with the aid of Zeb and a crutch, make his way about the room. His fractured ankle had not entirely healed. At times his head throbbed and pained till tears came into his eyes and blinded his vision. Across the small of his back, where the iron hoof of Fast Asleep struck, there were still dull aches. His whole body, yet sore, was in many places black and blue with bruises.

His mind, however, had grown perfectly clear, and neither its qualities nor energies were impaired. He was, therefore, often occupied with thoughts. Thoughts not entirely pleasant; indeed, rather bitter. Notwithstanding the fact that he had nearly seven thousand dollars, all his own, secure in the library safe; despite the fact that he was surrounded and attended by the kindest friends he had ever known; that he lived in a large house, in luxury, whose mistress was his constant and solicitous companion; that his health and strength were being rapidly restored; that his opportunities for a future were now beyond his wildest dreams, he was not happy.

He was annoyed, and his heart was heavy. The memory of the loving Phœbe was always present. He could not, though he often tried, banish her from his mind. In his heart he loved her in spite of her silence. Now that the purposes of his life appeared easy to accomplish, he discovered that his enthusiasm for their fulfillment was waning. His great object in being somebody was to please Phœbe, to have her admire him, to have her be proud of him.

If he was not to have her, never to see the look of admiration in her eye, never hear the voice of praise from her tongue, then he saw no purpose in being either great or good, wise or wealthy. Without the companionship of the idol of his heart, he felt that sooner or later his dreams, like all dreams, would remain figments of the air. To him there was no other, there could be no other whose influence could so completely kill, or thoroughly revive, the ambitious plans he had marked out for the future.

Day by day, Josephine Bowers had put off telling him of the interview she had with Phineas Strong, while he lay unconscious in the presence of both. She began, now, however, to see that she could not longer refrain from disclosing some account of the event. To tell the truth, she was sure, would result in Robbie's immediate departure for Viriginia. To tell a lie might result in the same thing, and yet she was confident that Robbie was a lad of too much spirit to intrude himself upon the society of those to whom his presence was distasteful.

Therefore, a lie, just a little invention, might after all keep him forever by her side. She resolved to tell a lie; to invent and relate if necessary the very opposite of what was true. She would take the chance.

There was some excuse for Josephine Bowers. For ten years she had led a barren life—that is, barren of those sweet results which women love to imagine are the sure rewards for wifely constancy, domestic devotion. So far her life had been a failure. In her heart the responsive feeling which every wife should have for her husband was totally wanting. She respected Judge Bowers, and in public was rather proud to be seen in his company as his wife. His wealth, his judicial position, his probity, and his learning were all calculated to arouse the envy of her less fortunate friends; and for years this was, to her mind, ample compensation for the sacrifice of sentiment. But now this novelty and charm had faded; become insipid, tasteless. Social obligations bored, annoyed her. Her face was wreathed in smiles, but her heart was covered with crape. To her, long ago, had come the conclusion that life, without love, was a tame, yet restless existence. The human heart, lacking the other heart to beat responsive to its own, failed in its sweetest functions, was dead to tender impulses.

It has been noted that the recent misfortune of being the wife of an insane husband was regarded by her as having been brought about by the hand of God, for her especial benefit. It never occurred to her that God could just as well have killed him as driven him mad.

Inasmuch, therefore, as God had helped her so much to attain the object of her passion, surely He would not be displeased if she undertook now to help herself.

That she should fall in love with this young and brilliant Virginian, was, after all, rather to be expected. He was physically a handsome fellow. His disposition, always genial, inspired the regard of all who met him. His mind, wonderfully receptive, had become stored with a vast amount of knowledge, and his conversation, embellished with a natural wit and seasoned with a gracious voice, made him always entertaining. His generosity, his bravery, were all known and highly praised. His position in the heart of Judge Bowers was so secure that it was common talk, based upon the judge's own remarks, that Robbie Porter would inherit much of his estate.

Kind mothers and flattering girls lavished much attention upon him, and he was ever a welcome guest at the homes of wealth and fashion. During his convalescence, mothers and daughters, with flowers or delicacies, called daily to inquire about him. The whole town still talked of his great race, and his miraculous escape from death. He was the hero of every girl who saw that tragic trotting heat. His noble act in driving for Judge Bowers, the certainty and dexterity of his horsemanship, made him the idol of ten thousand loyal hearts. He was a winner all around; his name and feat on every tongue, in every newspaper. His fortune, too, was made—made in a day.

In addition to winning nearly two thousand dollars,

Judge Bowers had given him five thousand, and had said to several before the tragedy that he was going to divide the whole sum received for Dewy Iris with the wonderful driver.

So, to the world, Robbie was an object of homage, of pride, of envy. When we consider all these things, when we consider the now peculiar position of Josephine Bowers, who had wormed from this boy the secret of his heart, do you very much wonder she resolved to tell a lie or two in order to detain him near her?

She loved him.

Her love blinded her sense of right, stilled her conscience, and nerved her tongue to lie. In the name of love, or religion, base and noble things are sometimes done.

CHAPTER XLV.

A SEPTEMBER sun threw its morning rays across the soft carpet in Robbie's room. Its beams were warm and bright, and filled the place with glory. Robbie sat up in bed, and Josephine Bowers adjusted an extra pillow at his back.

She set before him a tray crowded with tempting food. Every viand had been prepared by her own hand. They were all redolent with the delicate flavor of affection. The daintiness of the array reflected the exhausted ingenuity of love. A dying man, with the joys of heaven awaiting, or the terrors of hell threatening, would not have delayed to partake. The yellow cream, its surface broken with the bubbles of richness; the aromatic flavor, floating from a silver urn, of choice tea; the delicate china dish, heaped with a variety of late raspberries, the pride of Judge Bowers' horticultural achievements; the toast, browned like a chestnut hull; the lumps of loaf sugar in a bowl of silver, lined with gold, of filagree edge and chased exterior; the thin slices of ham, parboiled and broiled, sprinkled with herbs, and flanked at either end with an egg, big, white, round and yellow, emitting under his nostrils the blended flavor of ham and eggs, and delighting his artistic eye with the perfect symmetry of their arrangement in an oval dish of solid silver; the snow-white napkin; the vase of fresh flowers; the jeweled hand that deftly buttered the toast, that poured the tea, that sugared the berries, and covered them with cream; that pushed aside his straying locks; the radiant face, often so near his own as to nearly touch the down that was now of luxurious growth; the eyes that looked into his; the voice that bade him eat; the red lips so near; the heaving bosom, rising and falling with the waves of perfume that floated from her person; the muffled rustling of her tasteful gown; the golden chains that jingled from the bracelets on her arms; that beautiful hair, with its graceful roll, adorned with its tortoise combs, falling in a bunch of curls, oiled, shining and long, upon her neck and back; the necklace at her throat, with its sparkling diamond and its golden heart; her graceful pose, and her tender touch, had a wonderfully strange effect upon Robbie. He was not wholly aware of it, but this woman was daily creeping into his heart and driving out the image of his beautiful Phœbe.

A repetition of the scene like the foregoing occurred almost every morning. At each recurrence Robbie became more uneasy, more embarrassed.

These two were often alone, and yet when alone seldom spoke. Between them a sense of restraint had come.

Mrs. Bowers was never happier, apparently, than in waiting upon her patient. She read to him, and brought him many books he had never seen. Among these was an edition of Byron's "Don Juan." Once she had tried to discuss with him the character of Julia. But he was too stupid to express any opinion.

He began gradually to understand this woman. He began also to realize that he was living on dangerous ground. He was natural, he was human, but he had to confess to himself that his nurse was a woman whose charms were daily growing. He liked her; was grateful beyond the art of language to express. He was ashamed of his feelings, but he wanted to hug her every time she came near him. He admitted, however, that he did not, could not, love her. His love was already fixed. He had given it once and given it all. But the animal passion—deny it if you want to—that pervades every human frame, was not lacking in our hero, and sooner or later he felt he would be false to his friend, the judge, false to Phœbe, false to himself. The thought was a horrible one, because the pride of virtue was his dearest boast. His mind was pure, his heart honorable, but, yes—but, temptation!

Opportunities were daily before him, and daily he strove to resist, to overcome their influence. His nurse, however, as he regained health, grew more ardent, more melting. She sighed as she stroked his hair, and her hand trembled when she poured the tea. He was going, he felt it. She was going, she knew it. He strove to ward off the danger; she redoubled her arts to increase it. He longed for strength to leave the house; she prayed that he might never recover, if his recovery meant his departure.

"You have never told me what Uncle Phineas said

when he was here.   Tell me now," he asked, one evening when they sat alone, and the growing dusk crept upon the scene.

"I wanted to spare you additional pain," she said tenderly.   Both felt the influence of the softening hour.

She drew her chair in front of the big, easy one in which he reclined, and continued, passing her soft hand soothingly over his pale one, that rested upon his knee: "Better not know it.   Forget," she went on, "you ever knew the Strongs, for——"

"Stop, please!"   He raised his hands.   "Don't say such things to me.   They are the best people that ever lived.   Phœbe is the sweetest woman that I ever knew!"

That settled it with Josephine Bowers.   Her qualms all fled at the last remark.   She spoke, and somewhat harshly:

"Oh, well, since you must be satisfied, I'll tell what he said, and then your eyes will be opened!"

"Go on," he said feebly.

"Well, your good uncle, of course stopped the runaway, but when the doctors told him you would die, he stood up, looked at you a minute, and said: 'Vengeance is mine, I will repay, sayeth the Lord!   He is better dead.   The girl he ruined is dead by this time. This is my reward for loving an ingrate!'"

Robbie was staring in speechless astonishment, and striving through the gloom to read the woman's face.

"Did he say those things?"

"Those were his very words."

He covered his face in his hands to hide the pain his heart reflected there.

"Oh, Mrs. Bowers," he moaned, "I have lost the best of friends; I have ruined the most lovely of all lovely characters. I am a villain, a base wretch, a scoundrel. No wonder he hates me now. They all hate me. I can never go back, never see her face again."

For a moment his emotion arrested her reply.

"I do not hate you," she said, leaning forward, so close he felt her warm breath upon his hands. "To me you are not a villain, but a splendid, noble, young man. Why mourn or lament the past? Have you not new and tried friends? Friends who overlook, forgive the past? Friends who nursed you back to life, who paid all your bills, who," she faltered, "who can do more for you, if you will, than your little Quaker sweetheart and her stern father could ever do. Come," she continued, pushing his hands from his tear-wet face, "cheer up! We all make mistakes in early life. I have made mine, and have suffered. I am trying to forget the past; have forgotten it. I am looking to the future. Its prospects give me present happiness. The future is bright for you. You can be every thing you wish. Regain your health, complete your studies, enter the profession of the law. Applause will ring in your ears. Laurels will fall at your feet. Love will worship at your shrine, and wealth will increase your power."

She was glowing now with enthusiasm, and the radiance of her face made a halo before his own.

"There is no love for me!" he answered sadly.

"Oh, yes, there is!" She began to stammer, hesitate. Her eyelids dropped, her color heightened; the scene affected her. The faint odors of the room, his presence so near, his grief, the glamor of a passion she had never before known, the yearnings for the first time of a heart heretofore a stranger to the mystic spell of love, all awakened emotions the darkness did not entirely conceal. Robbie was suddenly aware that a terrible struggle was raging in the breast that heaved before him. She was trying to continue, and yet trying to repress her speech. Whether what she wanted to express came out I do not know, but her lips parted, and in a half-stammer, half-whisper, he heard—his ears did not deceive him: "I—I—love you!"

Convulsively she had seized his two hands and held them in her own.

The darkness fell upon them. The silence was such that each heard the heart of the other. The power of speech and action had left both. Robbie was not wholly surprised; he half-expected just such a scene to occur. He was gaining a little knowledge of the world, and came to the conclusion that Josephine Bowers' conduct toward him was very much the same as that of his adored Phœbe.

He was not wholly a stranger to sighs, glances, and the lingering, gentle pressure of the hand. There were, however, two considerations against yielding to his natural impulses. He did not try to withdraw his hands, for if he had, his arm would have stolen around her waist, and he would have kissed her in spite of himself. Memories of Phœbe crowded rapidly before him, and his respect for his demented friend in a padded cell at Norristown rose before him like a wall. The woman turned her face upward, and half-expected he would kiss her.

He did not. He found speech.

His estimation of the goodness of Josephine Bowers was gone.

Slowly he raised himself and pushed her gently from him.

"Don't!" he said kindly, "don't make me forget all sense of honor. Don't talk to me of love. Don't do anything to make me lose my good opinion of you. Don't make me ashamed to meet my friend and benefactor, your husband. Oh, Mrs. Bowers, my heart is dead, and my hopes die with it. I am all that I said and more. I am an ungrateful wretch. I wish I could honorably take you in my arms, for I have long known that your married life was barren of love. I understand, and Heaven knows I pity you. Your lot is more miserable than my own."

"You understand?" she said at last, in a bewildered way. "Then you can sympathize, and forgive my unwomanly actions. You know what love is. I also know now."

"Yes!" he went on slowly. "I know too well, but Heaven will never bless yours or mine with its smiles. Mine is already buried in ashes. I hope yours won't end in despair."

His words, his manner, had called her back to calmness. She was natural now, but did not rise.

"You will forgive me?" she asked. "Don't think ill of me? We will be friends always?"

She arose, extended her hand. "Good-night!"

She gave him an impulsive kiss and fled.

She was older in the art of love than Robbie. Her heart beat wildly as she sped along the hall to her own room.

"Before another month," she said mentally, "he will forget the name of Phœbe Strong, and will tell me so."

Her kiss on Robbie Porter's mouth had an electric effect. It shattered his adamant resolutions, and instinctively he stretched his arms to enclose her form.

His surprise made his action slow.

She was gone!

He never saw her face again. With her went the influence which she seemed exercise over him.

His feelings underwent a complete revulsion.

"This must never occur again!" he thought; "and yet there is no way to prevent it. One more touch of that hand, one more kiss, and honor will fly out of the window!"

It was inevitable. Long he thought of the situation, and long he planned a solution of the difficulty.

There was but one way. He would leave the house forever. It was cowardly to run away, but that was the only thing to do. He was in no condition to travel, still lame, still weak. He was resolved, however, to go, and to go that night. There was but one way to do this. That was to take Zeb into his confidence. With his help he could reach the depot, take the midnight train for the West, and in the morning be hundreds of miles away from temptation, where new scenes, new faces, would, perhaps, banish thoughts no longer pleasant.

Zeb was hard to persuade, but a ten-dollar bill won him over. He assisted Robbie to dress, helped him to the library, where, while he went for the horses, Robbie opened the iron safe, and took therefrom his package of money. Drawing himself to the table, and turning up the gas light, he took a pen and wrote:

"DEAR MRS. BOWERS: The scenes of to-night would soon be repeated. Your reputation, your peace of mind will be less disturbed by my absence. Your kindness, I know, is illy repaid, but some day, in another way, I may show you how deeply sensible I am of your devotion. The world will call me what I am, a fool, but my conscience will not upbraid me. Honor and wealth are yours. I cannot deprive you of the former; of the latter I have no need. My hope is to escape the memory of everything I have ever known. With this end in view, I will travel. Be happy! Farewell.
"Yours,   ROBERT PORTER."

He inclosed it, wrote her name on the envelope, and put it in his pocket.

Zeb helped him to the carriage, and returned for a traveling bag, into which he had hastily thrown a few clothes.

There were few Western travelers that evening, and he secured sleeping car accommodations to Chicago.

"The end of the line," the ticket seller said. He gave a ten-dollar bill to Zeb, placed the letter in his hands, and bade farewell to the city of Lancaster.

How relieved he felt, as a full sense of what he had done came upon him. Unexpectedly to himself, in spite of the jarring and rumbling under him, he fell asleep, and did not awake till the train was well into the State of Ohio.

CHAPTER XLVI.

IT was a little late when Josephine Bowers, arrayed the next morning in one of those fetching gowns, smelling of the bath, and exhaling perfume at every step, appeared at the breakfast table. She was radiant with smiles, and gracious beyond precedent. She finished the meal, when Zeb, hat in hand, entered and handed her the letter. He was going immediately to depart, but a scream arrested his purpose, and the sound of a falling body striking the floor caused him to fly to the side of his mistress. The letter was clasped in her hand. Zeb dashed water in her face, lifted her gently to the sofa, and fanned her vigorously till her eyes opened.

"Who helped him from the house?" she demanded, almost in a rage.

"I did," Zeb replied.

"Did he say where he was going?"

"Everywhere! Said he would never stop travelin' as long as he had a cent!"

A groan came from the lips of the unhappy woman.

With a struggle she arose, steadied herself a moment, and in a hoarse-like voice said: "Zeb, say nothing of this. Did he take his clothes?"

"Yes, a few, missus."

"Pack the rest in a box and ship them to Phineas Strong, Fredericksburg, Virginia. Never mention his name again, Zeb!"

She swept from the room. It was days ere her face was seen again. Then few knew her. From her eyes had gone their liquid tenderness; color had left her face, and over it had stolen an expression of settled melancholy—suffering. She rarely spoke; she never smiled. She had had her romance; she had now to bear her cross.

Her first day of grief gave way to revenge, and she wrote the cruel letter apprising Phineas Strong of the death of Robbie Porter. After that the terrors of remorse haunted her mind, and clung to her all the days of her life.

Her chickens had all come home to roost.

Robbie Porter, still half-invalid, but pleased at his freedom, was more happy than he had been for many days. Phœbe was gone; of that there could be no doubt. She despised him, and Uncle Phineas must also execrate his memory. His heart yearned toward them all. Had he yielded to its promptings, he would have been on his way to River View. But pride, that stubborn pride, which first wooed him from that hospitable roof, urged him further away. So he shut up his breaking heart, consigned the memory of Phœbe to its innermost recesses, swept his forehead with his hand, and said: "I will forget her!"

Thus he resolved, but daily broke his resolution for twenty years.

He awoke the next morning in Chicago, but its smoke, wooden houses and wooden sidewalks had no charms for him. He did not want to stop anywhere. To go, to get away from everywhere, from everything, even beyond the borders of civilization, was his hope, his desire. He believed he could ride away from his own thoughts, and leave in their wake reflections, memories of days, scenes, places and faces that now were, he believed, doomed to utter oblivion.

He was mistaken, but it took years to make him confess his error.

CHAPTER XLVII.

JUDGE BOWERS died in an insane asylum.   His last words were: "Put not your trust in horses!"

His widow never remarried.   She shut herself up in the big house her husband left her, and in a few years became a spare, wrinkled old woman.

Dewy Iris trotted races, but never beat her Lancaster record.

Robbie Porter recovered entirely his pristine strength of body and mind, and in a few years, traveling from place to place, apparently forgot, in the fascination of that infinite variety the novice ever finds, the melancholy incidents of his earlier life.

It is no part of my story to follow him in all of his wanderings.   He was true to his words to Zeb.   He stopped only when his money was exhausted.   He was, however, satisfied.   He had seen most of the world, and returned at last to his native land.

Now the charms of travel were gone.   A longing for rest, and a semi-reviving of his earlier dreams took possession of him.   He would renew his studies, try for admission to the bar, and woo ambition to his breast. During his travels his taste for reading clung to him as of old, and in three years he had devoured a vast number of books on all conceivable subjects.   His mind had broadened, and his conversational powers had wonderfully enlarged. He was rich in reflections, posted in art, literature, and the ways of the world, but totally lacking in everything necessary to make a living. His resolution to stop going came to him while crossing the State of Iowa. It was in the early autumn, and the rich fullness of the country appealed to his remaining notions of the practical.

He had made the acquaintance of a fellow-traveler, a plainly-dressed man, with a placid face, a soft voice and an easy manner. He looked like a well-to-do farmer or stock raiser. He was both. His conversation indicated intelligence, and expressed philosophy. Robbie interested him, and his stories of travel so impressed him that he begged Robbie to honor him with his company, and quit the train at the next stop, a few miles west of Burlington. Robbie consented.

The two exchanged confidences, and formed a friendship that continued for years. The gentleman chanced also to be a school director, and had that day been to a distant town in search of a teacher to take the district school for the coming term. Before they had reached his home, he had offered Robbie the place at a salary of sixty dollars a month, saying at the same time: "You can board with me for ten dollars a month."

Here was a chance, and Robbie accepted on the spot.

He taught this school four years, and his name is no doubt remembered to this day by pupils long since fathers and mothers. His spare time was devoted to law books, and diligently, faithfully, he employed it.

He moved into town, opened a law office, and his friend, the school director, gave him his first case.

A law practice in a country town, however, is not apt to afford as many opportunities for prominence and wealth as a large city, and his business was, after all, illusive in its promises and uncertain in its remunerative features. It had one redeeming quality, it involved nearly every variety of jurisprudence, so that, if the country attorney has business, he is bound to become a better all-round lawyer than his city brother, the scope of whose practice is too often limited to specialties.

Robbie's qualities brought him his share of the litigation, and in general the confidence and admiration of many friends. He was often successful, and frequently acquitted himself with distinction. He became known as a dangerous adversary in a case, and his services were generally sought by people whose chances of success were often desperate.

Robbie, however, had never been taught, and had never formed strict business habits. He was a trifle indifferent, often late in his appointments, frequently tardy to appear in court, and in many ways annoying to clients, whose nervousness in litigation became intensified at the calm, passive, phlegmatic way he proceeded with their affairs, or tried their cases.

Then, too, if he lost the suit his coolness, indifference, if you please, was aggravating. He simply said, "Both sides can't win," and walked smiling and happy from court.

Sometimes, too, when he had been successful, and collected a fee, he closed his office, tacked a card on the door, "Out of town," and disappeared from view. Search or inquiry for him were alike useless. No one knew where he had gone or when he would return. His absences were generally determined by the amount of the fee. Sometimes he was gone six days, and sometimes six weeks. He would return, though, smiling and happy, and in a few days his genial ways would draw around as of yore his old clients, his fond admirers. But his practice was of a desultory character, and he had gradually grown tired of it. He became less studious, and less attentive.

As a means for a livelihood he was compelled to pursue his calling. His temporal wants supplied, his ambition waned, and I verily believe had not his necessities required it, he would have been content to recline in the shade of a tree, and read and reread his favorite authors. He was known as the happiest fellow in town, and his philosophy taught him the folly of discontent.

From religious gatherings and social functions he had long since withdrawn. His sweetest companions were his silent books, his faithful dog, his dextrous rod, and his unerring gun.

In this way ten years passed. He was getting along in life now, and was little richer than when he quit the country school.

He had longed to get away from the place, and had for some time been planning his departure.

In court was pending a case involving the title to large tracts of land. Robbie was one of several counsel employed. It became necessary to take the testimony of witnesses living in New York City. He made his trip, examined the witnesses, saw that the commissioner forwarded the depositions, and wrote to his friend the school director that he would never return. The testimony he elicited would win his case. He therefore instructed his friend to sell his effects and forward the proceeds to New York. Six weeks among the pleasures and palaces of the mighty metropolis won him completely. His life in the West he now regarded as wasted.

Under the impulse of the busy scenes he daily witnessed his enthusiasm revived. He fondly imagined that the great dreams of his earlier years would here be realized. There were already six thousand other lawyers in the city of New York, and he was a total stranger. Nevertheless, he entered the lists, and in a few weeks a window of a big building on Broadway was adorned with golden letters that read "Robert Porter, Attorney-at-Law."

His fee from the West, with the proceeds of a rather large library, enabled him to furnish his present offices with necessary and attractive appointments.

The novelty in the various attractions of metropolitan life for a year or so afforded him delight and entertainment. He became a patron of the theater, a buyer of books, a lover of music, a tasteful and expensive dresser, and a good liver.

One year, however, was sufficient to exhaust most of
the charm in the life he was leading. He grew tired
of the crowds, the never-ending roar of traffic, the glare
of the footlights, and the smirking social set in which
he moved.

He made aquaintances, and some business came from
their associations, but old habits, long ago formed,
clung to him, and he attended to the demands of his
profession only when the exigencies of his exchequer
absolutely required. The result of his lax method
therefore soon brought him to that financial condition
which one finds so common among the dwellers in large
cities. The needs of the present day were sufficient.
"Take no thought of the morrow," became his philosophy, and the days and weeks glided away as to him,
serene as an unruffled sea.

To those who claimed to know him best, he seemed
like a man whose past had no regrets, whose present
was entirely happy, and whose future was without ap-
prehension. With him all seasons were summer, and
every hut a palace; and yet he was without fortune,
without position. He had neither political purposes
nor social aspirations. Admittedly able in his profession and brilliant in debate, he was nevertheless modest
and retiring. He sought nothing, desired nothing.
For him the world had already done all it could, all he
demanded. He had seen its every part, and enjoyed
all its beauties, partaken of all its charms. He had his
romance, won his love and lost it. His longing for
travel had been gratified, his desire of fortune more

than satisfied. His ambition, once a wild, boyish dream, to be a lawyer, was achieved. Even his passion for books was beginning to wane. He had read so many now, and the good ones were all familiar, the necessity for rereading them no longer remained.

In the merciless, heartless conditions of a great city his generosity, his charity, his good impulses were unimpaired. No man questioned his honor, and no client ever doubted his fidelity. Therefore, it was nearly true that in looking over the vista of the passing years, he might well be content. All of his purposes in life had been achieved. He had become an educated, refined gentleman, identified with the noblest of all noble professions—a profession which involves the collected wisdom of ages, in which the glory of Lycurgus still exists, in which the brilliancy of Cicero is still shining; a profession in which oratory has climbed the "imperial heights," and pathos has touched the saddest chords; a profession which is the avenue to the loftiest places that man may reach in kingdom or republic. Cæsar was a lawyer, so was Lincoln. Cæsar's star still shines; Lincoln's sun will never set.

If a man in life achieves nothing else than to become an honored member of a profession which has developed more genius, more wit, more eloquence, more learning, more heroes, than all other professions combined, he cannot pass away from earth without sensations of pride, without feelings of joy. So then, if our hero was a happy man, there were many things to make him so. He had health, friends, could gratify his temporal wants, and indulge in the sweet extravagances and little luxuries of life.

True, he had to some extent become a man of the world. He took his pleasures where he found them, and his philosophy afforded plausible arguments for his conduct. He mingled with the gay, and was sometimes the delightful companion of the revelers of the night.

Indeed, for ten years now his life had been such that he even deluded himself with the reflection that he was a contented and a happy man.

He was not.

He lived a lie, and by a smiling face concealed the ashes of his buried hopes. He had said nearly twenty years before that he would forget Phœbe Strong. It was the one thing in his life he could not do.

He failed.

In this failure, reader, was the secret of his unknown position in the world. This failure, of which his friends knew nothing, was the real reason he never heard the trump of fame. For fame without Phœbe was nothing. This failure was the real reason that wealth had no allurements. Without Phœbe, what need had he of money? It was this failure that warped his industry, stifled his ambition, paralyzed his energies, and made his life like the heart within him, slow, impassive, sluggish, dead to opportunities, unmoved by consequences.

The gilded theater, the smiles of the siren, the sparkling wine, the crowded street, the gay parks, the shining sea, the silent woods, the rolling hills, the sparkling streams, the lonely bower, the early morn, the dewy eve, the fields and flowers of summer, and the ice and snow of winter, had all been associated and mixed in his life of pleasure. He never indulged in the diversions of either but the face of Phœbe Strong came to him, sometimes with a sad, reproachful look, sometimes with the sweet smile of love and the glow of affection.

In the silence of his chamber, in the stillness of the night, he heard her voice. In dreams he saw those wondrous eyes, touched those moist red lips with his own, and felt her warm white arms upon his breast, around his neck. Heavens! how real were some of these dreams! How often would he suddenly awake, stretch forth his arms, murmur, "Phœbe, Phœbe!" and when the consciousness that it was all a dream came fully upon him, that only an impalpable vision had flitted near, express the sigh that comes from aching hearts, and in melancholy memories, in a silence almost oppressive, strive again to bury recollections, which though hallowed were no longer sweet.

Thus he lived, and yet he met the morning sun with a smiling face, and in the eyes of the world passed for a light-hearted, happy man. But Byron says:

" They mourn, but smile at length, and smiling mourn,
  The tree will wither long before it fall,
  The hull drives on though mast and sail be torn,
  The roof-tree sinks but molders on the hall

In massy hoariness; the ruined wall
Stands when its wind-worn battlements are gone,
The bars survive the captive they enthral,
The day drags through, though storms keep out the sun
And thus the heart will break, yet brokenly live on."

He did not care to confess it, but these lines often forced themselves upon him and were mentally repeated again and again.

He could not live down his early love, he could not forget the sweet face that inspired it. In the fullness of his physical power, in the intellectual scope of his mental vigor, he knew the handicap that checked the full completion of his life's purposes. He knew now the lasting influence, the priceless treasure of a first love. In twenty years Wandering the wide world over, seeing daily now the faces of ten thousand smiling maidens, he beheld none like the face of Phœbe Strong. Sometimes he would walk from Battery Park to Central Park, a long distance, reader, along that thoroughfare, whose pavements daily re-echo the tread of a million hurrying feet, whose dazzling shops bewilder the stranger, and whose tall buildings, the tops of which are lost in floating clouds, reflect the daring genius, the lofty conceptions of ambitious men.

What a moving panorama of human faces Broadway always presents to the student of human nature. The variety is infinite, the expressions countless. All the passions of the human heart are reflected in the smiles and wrinkles that pass constantly before your gaze. Hope is there, so is despair. Love is there, so is hate.

There is expectancy, here realization. Here is fortune, there is poverty. Here is the bounding spring of
youth, the halting steps of age. Here is the Sister of
Charity, and there the courtesan of crime; side by side
they press amid the struggling throng. The lawyer
with his bag of briefs, the broker with his bunch of
stocks, the ragged urchin, and the little Lord Faunt-
leroys, the preacher and the reporter the hod carrier
and the dude, all there, rushing like mad,   elbowing,
pushing in a never-ending procession.

Above Fourteenth Street begins that brilliant display of fair faces, fine feathers, gorgeous gowns, and
the kaleidoscope of changing colors. On warm, sunny
days this part of Broadway for a mile or more is redolent with the rich aromas that exhale from the rustling silks of fashion's favorites.

Jewels sparkle, bright eyes grow brighter, animation is
in every countenance, broad ribbons flutter in your face,
feathered plumes, black and white, red and green, in
graceful waves, in inextricable confusion, dangle before
you. Upon this panorama, in which art and nature
exhibited their choicest works, Robbie would often
gaze, sometimes searchingly, and mentally wonder why
in all that lovely collection of female loveliness he never
saw his Phœbe's form and face. He never wended his
way through this chattering crowd but his mind, involuntarily, perhaps, conjured up memories of her goodness, her beauty. He began at last to believe that some
day, in that moving mass, he would see her. Then he
indulged in delightful reveries over the imaginary meet-

ing.   Once his thoughts crystallized into verse, which
he wrote down.   Under the caption, "If you should see
a face," the following lines he sent to a great newspaper for publication.   They were never printed, but as
they express better than I can the secret longing
of their author's heart, I insert them here:

" If within the crowd's mad throng,
 That daily rush the streets along,
 If among the feathered, gay dressed fair,
 You should some day see wandering there,
 The face, the sweet, sweet face of long ago,
 Of one, the one, the very one, whom you did know
 Belonged to you.   How would your own become aglow,
 With light and love.
 How quick the heart beat, as you strove,
 Right there and then, despite of chattering tongue
 And wondering men,
 To reach her side,
 And stop the rising sigh on those sweet lips,
 By pressing fondly to your own,
 And in the waiting ear,
 With tender words, exclaim:
 At last! At last! it is my Phœbe dear!"

CHAPTER XLIX.

ROBBIE was nearly forty now. He had climbed the hill in life, and was going down the slope. In his physical attractions, the manly vigor of youth still lingered. The glow of health was in his cheeks, and his eyes reflected the quiet tenderness of a generous heart. His face, always illumed with the light of intelligence, was bright, kindly, winning; nevertheless, silver streaks were creeping among those chestnut locks, and old Time was drawing a few semi-wrinkles across that broad and shining brow.

With the approach of age came increased indifference. Why not? He was alone in the world. His needs were few; there was not to his knowledge one human being that could claim him by consanguinity or affection. Most of his past had been forgotten. He forgot his mother, forgot his father, forgot his battle scenes, banished Aunt Rachel and Phineas Strong from his mind, shut out the memory of Josephine Bowers, relegated his friend, the judge, to mental oblivion, and gradully formed his chief source of contentment in the reflection that he stood alone in the big round world.

To his friends he laughingly sometimes likened himself to a mule, for it had neither pride of ancestry nor hope of posterity. It was his boast that he was just

Robert Porter; that he began nowhere, and would
eventually end at the same place.   His philosophy had
brought him to that condition in which he had no hope
of heaven and no fear of hell.   Whether there was or
was not a God no longer disturbed the serenity of his
mind.   Earth might again run red with war, and revo-
lutions might have crumbled the political fabric of
his country to dust, he would have sat, calm, serene,
unmoved amid the slaughter and the wreck.   Whether
man lived after he died or died eternally after he lived
had long since ceased to awaken thought or inspire conversation.

For the science of the law he had still some venera-
tion, but he was beginning to doubt even the utility of
this complex and uncertain system.   He saw too often
it was the creature of wealth, and the instrument of
power.   Left to his own impulses, he would have retired from its practice, and without a dollar returned to
those delicious and fragrant scenes of his Virginia
home, where he thought the music of the rippling
river would lull him to repose, and the songs of birds
would awaken him to innocent harmony.   There he
could behold, with never-tiring pleasure, the green
hills rolling in the distance, and the tall pines that
gracefully grew upon their verdant sides.   "There,"
he thought, "the clang of commerce will never mar my
repose, and the roar of traffic will never disturb
my reveries!"

.   .   .   .

On the 30th of April, 1890, a little after the noon

hour, Robbie Porter stood in the rotunda of the Astor House. He had just lunched, and was proceeding to the street, when the knowledge that a sudden shower was falling arrested his attention. His office was but a little way up Broadway, and he might have, by hurrying, arrived there without much damage to his wardrobe. But Robbie never hurried, and it was the most unlikely thing that he should hurry in a rainstorm. So he stood near the double doors and peered through their swinging glasses upon the dripping crowd that rushed in groups up and down the street.

He picked his teeth with calmness and content. His florid face, and rounded vest suggested health, and reflected plenty. His dress, new, modern, perfect fitting, fastidious, bespoke the man of taste. In his immaculate, polished linen, his modest neckwear, his closely cropped hair, and clean-shaven face, neatness was completely expressed. His silk hat was of the latest pattern, and shone in its new polish, despite the cloudy day. His patent leather shoes, devoid of cracks, dust or dirt, reflected their brilliancy around the wet and muddy floor.

It had long been his custom to dine at this still famous hotel. Here he often met Western friends, and in the glories of a "mint smash" or a gentle "toddy," recalled the scenes of other days. He saw no friends this day, however, and waiting patiently for an abatement of the rain, lost himself in reverie. The swinging doors swung unnoticed, and the coming and going forms no longer attracted his attention.

A familiar slap on the shoulder and a merry voice aroused him. A tall gentleman had approached, and in enthusiastic words was saying:

"Just the man, by hookey, that I wanted to see. Been to your office; been over to Farrishes', been everywhere! How are you, old fellow?"

Robbie turned and recognized a newspaper friend, Harry Cullen, for whom he had often transacted business in the West.

"Good," he answered. "Glad to see you, old man. In town long?"

"Oh, yes, been here a year."

"In business?"

"Yes! Meant to hunt you up; somebody told me you were here, but busy, my boy, busy. Will you take a case? I've got one for you. You're the man of all others that can handle it. By Jove, it's lucky I found you. Not too busy, I hope, to take it, are you?"

"No," said Robbie. "Pretty busy, but for a friend, you know, guess I can crowd it in. What is it, murder, arson or breach of promise?"

"Breach of promise all right, but not the kind you mean. Married yet, old man?"

"No!" answered Robbie. "You are, I suppose?"

"Yes, married long ago, got two or three, yes, three children—that's right; got to buy shoes for the third one to-day. Do you know, Bob, children always want shoes! Buy shoes for my kids regularly every week. And eat! Mercy on me, old man! Never get married. My three young ones eat nine, yes nine, nine loaves of bread every day of their lives. But," he rattled on, "where can I explain this case to you?"

"Right here," said Robbie.

"No, come let's go right across to Park Row. Got my office over there, and I'll explain it all. Introduce you to your client, a woman! Oh, you needn't hold back. It's an old maid, gray, wears glasses. Come!"

"Don't care about getting my hat wet," said Robbie, making no move to go.

"Oh, damn your hat!" said Cullen. "Get this case and buy a new one. This is a good case, old man. Just like getting money from home. Wake up, you old fossil, and get a move on you. I've got an umbrella, anyhow."

He produced an article made of silk, and arm in arm the two left the hotel.

Cullen proceeded to tell that he was in the advertising business, and that his partner was a bright woman, named Miss Potter, a friend of his wife's, who formerly taught school in Philadelphia.

To her Robbie was presently introduced in this fashion by the bombastic Cullen:

"Now, Miss Potter, this is my friend, Bob Porter. Best fellow that ever lived. Knew him in the West— straight as a string—won't rob you. Good lawyer! Tell him all about that case of yours. He'll handle it just right, won't sell you out—fight for you till the cows come home and then give you all the milk. Treat him as you would a brother. Just sit right down, Bob, and listen."

Robbie, smiling, took the offered chair by the lady's side and remarked: "Mr. Cullen has a brilliant fancy and is of a romantic imagination. Permit me to listen to your tale of woe."

Miss Potter was a tall person, spare in flesh, neat, but rather severe in costume, and on her face time had already made some ravaging marks. She was, however, pleasing in her manner, and cordial in her acknowledgment of the introduction.

"It is just like this, Mr. Porter. Mr. Cullen has told you, no doubt, we are in the advertising business. Well, sometimes I go out and make advertising contracts. One of my customers, a millinery firm up Broadway, very heavy importers, with customers all over the country, wanted an elaborate description of their spring styles published in a few of the daily papers, exclusively as a news article, that is, a 'write-up,' you understand. Well, we solicited and secured the contract. I personally prepared the article. It was published in the *World* and *Herald* last Sunday a week ago. Here are the copies. The contract provided for payment when the work was completed. It called for four thousand lines of pure reading matter. There are the articles. We have presented the bill and they have refused payment."

"Why?" asked Robbie.

She took up one of the papers, and pointing to the bottom of a column where the article concluded, showed the letters "adv." in small characters.

"And that indicates?"

"That is the sign that the article is a paid advertisement."

"Well?"

"They claim that mark vitiates their contract, and injures the value of the write-up."

"Was the contract in writing?"

"Certainly."

"Let me see it."

She produced a rectangular-shaped piece of paper, about four inches wide and ten inches long. On one side was written and printed the following:

"NEW YORK, April 16, 1890.

"To MESSRS. CULLEN & POTTER:

"You are hereby authorized to insert our advertisement to occupy four thousand lines of reading matter, two thousand lines to appear in the edition of the New York *World*, of Sunday, April 20, 1890, and two thousand lines in the edition of the New York *Herald* of Sunday, April 20, 1890, for which upon publication thereof we agree to pay to you or your order four thousand dollars ($4,000).

"BLOOM & BLOOM,
"687 Broadway,
"New York."

"Make out your bill and write me an order that I am your agent, authorized to collect this account," said Robbie.

"Can you make them pay?" she queried doubtingly.

"They will pay it before the sun sets!" he said quietly.

"What did I tell you?" broke out Cullen, coming over to where they sat. "There's a man that knows his business. Give him the account. You'll just chew them fellows up, won't you, Bob? Damn people, always trying to get out of their contracts. I'll tell you what we'll do, Bob, collect that account and we'll give you a fourth of it."

"All right!" said Robbie, folding up the two papers, the contract and bill together. "You wait here, and I'll either bring you this money before four o'clock or those merchants will get some advertising in the courts that won't help their credit."

"Good boy!" exclaimed Cullen, taking a Highland fling step or two. "Good boy, Bob! Oh, he's all right, Potter, don't you worry," he went on as Robbie departed.

In two hours he returned and handed to Miss Potter a check for four thousand dollars.

"By gad!" said Cullen, "I didn't think it could be done. "What'd you do to make them?"

"Oh, just gave them a little talk, a little law, a little common sense, and they wilted."

"Well done, indeed," said Miss Potter. "The way they talked to me and Mr. Cullen made us think we'd have a long fight to get that money."

"Oh, Bob's the best that ever came over. Can't get away from you, can they, old man? Draw a check for one thousand dollars to the order of Robert Porter," he went on, addressing a clerk. "There!" affixing his signature to the check, and handing it to Robbie.

"There, old boy, that will be good when the bank opens in the morning, just as soon as we make a deposit. Gad, old fellow, if the firm had lost that account it would have had to go out of business."

"Glad you're pleased," said Robbie.

"Pleased; why we're delighted. Don't go, Miss Potter has a case she wants to talk to you about; ten thousand in it, maybe."

"If I could have a moment's time with you?" said Miss Potter. "It's about mother's matter. Could you come over to our house some evening?"

"Why, yes, I guess so," said Robbie, whose experience with female clients had made him rather cautious about taking up their battles.

"Oh, I'll pay you," spoke up the lady, who imagined his hesitating manner was caused by the suspicion that there might be no remuneration in the proposed visit. "Can you come soon?"

"Any time you name."

"This evening?"

"If you want me, yes."

"The sooner, the better, as the matter now admits of no delay. If you can accompany me, we will go at once. We live in Jersey City, and it takes almost an hour to get to our home. I will undertake, if you will honor us with your company, to prepare a simple but palatable dinner."

Sarah Potter had already formed a most amazing opinion of the ability of Robbie Porter, and what was surprising to herself, a most decided liking. Instinctively she felt that she could trust him, and that of all others, he was the man to whom her mother might impart all her secrets in safety.

A good dinner, or the prospect of one, always appealed to Robbie, and he smilingly assured the lady he was at her service.

They left the office together, and in a few hours he was confronting memories that long ago were dead and buried. He was listening to a story more remarkable to his mind than all the pages of romance he had ever read.

Sarah Potter had presented him to a woman who must have been long past seventy. She was tall, spare, wrinkled. Her cheeks were hollow, her big black eyes were sunk behind eyebrows whose ghastly whiteness gave them a weird, unnatural look. Her hair, still abundant, was of the color of snow. Her voice, once perhaps sweet and low, was now a harsh, unnatural whisper. Her features, however, were regular and striking. The large eyes, the classic forehead, and finely turned chin, adorned as they once were with the animation of youth, the color of health, must have made her a wonderfully beautiful woman. But now, her wasted form, her thin hands, the deathlike pallor of her face, and an expression of half-terror, all sorrow, robbed her of nearly every charm. There are old faces, still beautiful, peaceful, happy, lighted with hope, beaming still with expectancy. Such was not hers. In those eyes was no light of hope. Instead, they seemed to reflect the gloom of despair. Hers was a face over which once the hot passions of the human heart had raged, and left it seared, seamed and broken. Only tragedy, deep grief, great sins, jealous rage, infinite hate, blasted love, produce such faces. In that face, Robbie read all of these. Instinctively he felt that he was about to hear the story of a woman's life in which all the contending passions would play a part. He was not mistaken.

The dinner concluded, and all being composed about a hearthstone fire, for it was still cold without, Sarah Potter reminded her mother that the lawyer had come to hear her story and take her case. She went on to say: "Mother is almost blind, but I am sure if she could see your face fully she would not hesitate. The matter would have long ago been attended to, but until this very day we have never felt that we could afford even the expense of investigation."

The old woman's first whispering took Robbie Porter off his feet, and he betrayed an interest, an emotion, quite unusual for a man who in twenty years had never experienced the sensation of surprise.

"To begin at the beginning, my maiden name was Lydia Langdon. My brother is the great Dr. Langdon, of Philadelphia. Perhaps you have heard of him?"

Robbie assured her that he once knew him well.

Then the memories of the race-track accident, and all of its horrible incidents flashed through his brain. Strange that there should be in Jersey City the agency in an old and ghostly woman to remind him of that melancholy scene.

She continued: "My conduct in early life estranged him, and we have not spoken in forty years. At sixteen I was an orphan. A distant relative offered me a home in Philadelphia. I became a member of the family, half-servant, half-companion, nurse girl, and seamstress. My relative, the husband, and head of the family, was a man nearly forty, tall, well-formed, handsome, generous. He treated me with tender and fatherly consideration. His wife and four sons composed the family. They were well-to-do, and lived in elegance and plenty. In religion they were Quakers. I had also been bred a Quakeress, so that I soon fell into their ways, and became a general favorite. Since the birth of their fourth son, the wife had been a victim of ill-health, and was frequently ordered to the country or the seaside. During one of these visits my patron made love to me. He was very handsome, and I was very young, very silly. I fell madly in love, and in a year gave birth to a child. His wife was at home, ill in bed, at the time. A realization of my shame, and a sense of the impending scandal, prompted me to attempt some plan to conceal disgrace, and protect him. I took my baby to the attic, where I knew was an old, small, empty hair-trunk. I put the little thing inside—a little girl—oh, so beautiful!—sprang the lock, and fled.

I reached my room, with its cries ringing in my ears.

That was fifty years ago, but I have heard that cry every night since. Overcome with nervousness and weak with excitement, I fainted. How long I remained unconscious I do not know, but when my senses came back, I was lying on the bed, and Phineas Strong was chafing my temples and rubbing my hands."

Robbie Porter was on his feet. He was staring at the old woman speechless, dumb.

"Pshaw!" he said to himself, sitting down.

"Pardon me, but my thoughts were far away." And then as if to reassure himself he asked:

"Whom did you say, please?"

"Phineas Strong," whispered the dry lips.

"Phineas Strong?"

She nodded her head affirmatively.

"Did you ever know him?"

"Yes, I knew him well. Go on, please."

"I told him what I had done. He was horrified. We both listened at the foot of the attic stairs, but the silence was unbroken. The little thing was smothered. It was now quite late and dark. I begged him to carry the trunk into the backyard, and bury it. He did it. He had just completed the task, and looked up. His wife had been watching him, and was standing by his side.

"Well, she found it all out. He told her everything. She forgave him on the condition that I should leave the house forever. I never saw his face again, but I would know it even now. She came to my room and told me I was an adulteress, a murderess. She said that I had robbed her of her husband, and as soon as morning came she would give me up to justice.

"There was only one thing that would save me—that was to disappear forever. I begged the woman I had wronged to spare my life. I waited not till morning, but when the house was quiet, arose, dressed, and God knows how I ever did it, fairly flew from the place. I was found unconscious on the street, and awoke in a hospital. My baby's plaintive cries still rang in my ears. Fever followed, and for a long while my life hung in the balance. I recovered, however. My brother found me and urged me to sue Phineas Strong. I refused. He took a pistol and went to his house, intending to kill him. The house was closed; the family had disappeared.

"My brother offered me a home with him. That I refused, and he became angry. I have never seen him since. I remained at the hospital and became a nurse.

"In my ward was a fair-haired, handsome man, in the last stages of consumption. I liked him very much, and he was constantly giving me presents of money. One day he asked me to marry him. His name was William Porter. He was from Virginia. He had killed his brother in a duel, he said, and had to leave the country. He said he owned a large estate, and had no living relative. If I would marry him, he would will his property to me.

"We were quietly married. At this time, though I did not know it, he was under contract to sell his property in Virginia. He went out one day, was seized with a hemorrhage, and bled to death before he could reach the hospital. On his person was found in bank bills nearly five thousand dollars. I did not know it then, but found out that on that very day he had given a deed for all his earthly possessions. I have since learned that the deed was not good without my signature, that I still have an interest in his estate. Is that true?"

"Perhaps," replied Robbie. "Is that all?"

Inwardly he felt that she had withheld some part of her story."

"No; but is not that enough?"

"Yes, for the purposes you desire; but your name is Potter now, and you married Porter. Tell me about that?"

"With the money my husband left I decided to travel, hoping, if possible, to escape the scenes and memory of my awful crime.

"I left the hospital, and with a matron who had been kind to me, sailed for Liverpool.

"Our ship went into a fog off the coast of Newfoundland, and we drifted upon the rocks. A young man whose acquaintance I made the first day out saved my life. We reached New Brunswick together. He was a fine-looking, genial fellow, and had once been a sailor. His name was Benjamin Potter. He expressed great liking for me. Out of gratitude for his goodness, I married him. We lived in Nova Scotia for several years. My daughter was born there. My husband purchased an interest in a coasting ship, and for two or three years fortune smiled upon us. One day, however, he and a few companions, half-starved, came home in a yawl boat. His vessel had been lost, with cargo, and most of the crew. From that day things went bad.   Finally we drifted back to Philadelphia. For ten years we endured all the pangs and privations poverty could bring.   A son was born to us, and our circumstances were such that I had to do nursing for a living, while my husband kept house and attended the children.   Things went wrong always with us.

"When the civil war broke out, my husband and the boy were in Delaware.   He enlisted in a volunteer regiment, and was immediately sent south.   My son, whom he had started home, never got there, and in a few weeks a letter from my husband told me the child had followed him to Washington.   My husband knew all about my marriage to Mr. Porter.   We both thought if I changed my name it might injure my chances of recovering his estate.   So, after coming to Philadelphia, we used the name of Porter.   He enlisted under that name.

"After the battle of Fredericksburg he wrote me that he was making inquiries about the Porter estate; to send him my marriage certificate and other papers; that Robbie was still with him—Robbie was the child's name."   The old lady was about to proceed, but stopped short upon dimly beholding the expression and attitude of her guest.

His face was almost bloodless; his lips parted, and his big round eyes fixed in a vacant stare.   With an effort he arose and leaned against the wall, his eyes still fastened upon the white-haired and shriveled form before him.   Slowly he raised his hand, and his voice came husky and choking:

"MY SON! DID YOU SAY MY SON?"

"You—need go—no further," he said. "I know the rest."

"Know it!" exclaimed mother and daughter in concert.

"Yes," said Robbie, "I know it better than you do.

"Your husband was the color bearer of the regiment. He was killed at Chancellorsville. I saw him die; I helped bury him; I can take you to his grave. He was buried on the farm of Phineas Strong, who bought it from a man named Porter. I am the boy 'Robbie.' I am your son."

Daughter and mother were on their feet. Surprise, doubt, wonder, incredulity, were in those eager faces.

"My son?" queried the mother, clutching at the mantel for support; "my son? Did you say my son?"

"Yes, there is no doubt of it. Look, both of you, look! Can't you see in me the willful Robbie Porter who played around the corner on Sansome Street; who ran away every day to sell the *Bulletin?* Don't you remember the blue and red anchor my father had tattooed on his left arm? Don't you remember he wrote you that I was shot in the leg at Fredericksburg? Don't you remember he wrote you about Major Lofland being killed; that his own trouser leg was torn off by a bursting shell?"

"Yes! yes!" the poor woman murmured. "Why, I have all the letters now.

"Sarah," tottering toward her daughter, "it is true! it is true! It is your brother! The grave has given up its dead. Oh, my son, my son! It seems so strange, like a dream, too good to be true—and you weren't killed?"

Robbie was deeply moved. His conscience condemned him. He walked to where the two women stood, and took them both in his arms.

"Mother, sister," he said, "forgive me! I was a wild boy, willful, disobedient, as you know. I was always in trouble when at home, always making mischief, and always being whipped by you, but never by father. I was, therefore, mostly with him.

"When he enlisted he put me on the boat, and told me to go home. He gave me a letter for you. Before the boat had reached Delaware River, I jumped overboard, swam ashore, and walked back to Wilmington. The regiment was gone. I carried a valise for a lady, who gave me a quarter. I put a three-cent stamp on the letter, dropped it in the post office, 'flipped' a freight train, and arrived in Washington a few hours after pap" (Robbie always referred to his father as pap). "At last they gave me a drum, a cap, and a pistol. A tailor in the company made me a suit of clothes, and I followed the army till pap was killed. He died within a mile of Phineas Strong's house. His daughter——"

"His daughter?" interrupted Mrs. Potter, looking up.

"Yes, his daughter, a beautiful young woman, found us in the big road. She took us both home. Father is buried there."

"Why," spoke up Sarah, smiling through her tears, "this is like a novel; seems more like fiction than fact."

"'Truth,'" said Robbie, "'is stranger than fiction.'

"Listen: the Strongs were Quakers. They treated me like I was a human being. I begged to be allowed to remain. They consented, and I grew to manhood there. I loved them, and was engaged to marry the daughter, and——"

"And what," questioned his sister, seeing that Robbie hesitated.

"Oh, no more. That is all. 'Whom first we love we seldom wed.'"

"And you didn't marry her?" asked the mother.

"No!"

"Why, that spoils the story," said Sarah. "What was the trouble?"

"Oh," replied Robbie, sighing deeply, "that is something I never found out."

"But you are married, of course," said Sarah.

"No!"

"Was it as bad as that?"

"It was a sincere attachment with me. I would marry her now if I could."

"Why not?"

"Well, that is another story. Let's to business.

"Mother," he said, "for you are my mother."

He was his old self now, and smiling.

"In fiction, it would, on an occasion of this kind, be expected that the long-lost son, the discovered daughter, and the new-found mother should fall into each other's arms, and with embraces, kisses, tears, make a scene. I never could affect a sentiment I did not feel.

I have never known a mother's love, a sister's care. This seems so like a dream to me, so unreal, so much like the invention of the novelist, that I am even now doubtful of its reality. However, I purpose to act just as though it were true.

"Mother, your life has been full of shadows. Mine has not been all sunshine. But from this on, let not your heart be troubled. As I remember you thirty years ago, your hair and eyes were black as coals. I recall now that settled look of trouble, but you were beautiful. Beauty may never come back, but happiness will. Phineas Strong and his wife Rachel are no doubt dead. There is not a living witness to accuse you of your crime. Forget it.

"Yours was the sin of youth; prompted by a wrong social system, inspired by false notions. Sorrow and grief such as yours would expiate a greater crime. Be happy! Smile! To-morrow we will start for Virginia. If you can prove that you are the wife of William Porter, you can claim an interest in River View."

"River View," she repeated. "That's the very name —the name my first husband told me the estate was called."

"Oh, I know it well," said Robbie. "There's not a foot of it I have not stepped upon. No doubt strangers live there now, but their title is clouded, and they will have to settle with you if they want it perfect."

"But how can I prove my marriage?"

"Oh, we'll find the proof. Get ready! We'll start to-morrow morning. Leave at eleven o'clock. We can be in Fredericksburg by six, and drive out to the place the next morning and see who claims to own it. We'll investigate a little. When I left there twenty years ago the place was worth thirty thousand dollars. It's probably worth fifty thousand now. Can you both be at the Pennsylvania depot to-morrow at eleven o'clock?"

"Yes," spoke up Sarah.

"All right," said Robbie. "I'll be there. I can get away now. Later I might not be able to go. Of course, if this is a dream, and we are all awake in time we won't go. It is now late."

He took his mother's cold and bony hands in his own, stroked them and kissed her tenderly. Sarah threw her arms around him, exclaiming:

"Mr. Cullen was right. You are the best that ever came over. Oh, we'll be proud of you."

He took up his hat. Mother and daughter urged him to remain overnight.

"No, I couldn't do it. Got to arrange some things to-night yet, and be up early. Don't fail to be on hand. No more sorrow after to-morrow. No more hard work; no more poverty, mother! Good-night, good-night, good-night," and he was gone.

CHAPTER L.

ROBBIE reached the street, surging with sensations better understood than described.

"Well," he exclaimed, as he boarded a car for the ferry, "I've read fiction, heard stories, but for a real dream in life this beats all! Wonder if I am awake. Must be. This is a street car—still I'll not believe it till I meet somebody I know, and ask them who I am."

He reached the New York shore and went straight to the Astor House bar. Before the crescent-shaped counter three or four men were talking. One of them was Harry Cullen. His hat was pushed back, his hands were waving, and his tongue was telling the incident of the Bloom & Bloom contract. Thrown over his arm, and attached by strings tied at the ends, hung a pair of shoes. Robbie walked up to the crowd, and without being observed, lifted one of the shoes, examined its size, then spoke:

"Cullen, is that the pair of shoes you were to buy for your child to-day?"

"Well, by G—d!" exclaimed Cullen. "Why, gentlemen, here's the man that did the business." He seized a half-filled glass of red liquor, resting on the counter, raised it high above his silk hat, and said:

"Gentlemen, drink to my friend, Robert Porter.

Here, barkeeper, set out that decanter and a glass. Take something, Bob. Why, man, you look like you have seen a ghost. What happened; old maid didn't propose to you, did she?"

"Gentlemen!" said Robbie, pushing his silk hat back, and wiping the perspiration from his forehead, "excuse me, but is this April 30, 1890?"

"What's left of it," said Cullen, glancing sideways at the clock over the cashier's booth.

Robbie had fished a piece of paper from his vest pocket, and unfolding it, passed it before his friend's eyes. "Is that a check for one thousand dollars?" "Why, yes," answered Cullen. "Look here, old man, have you come from a dope factory?"

"All right, then," replied Robbie. "I'll drink."

He swallowed half a glass of whisky, and continued, "Have one on me!"

All drank again.

"Cullen," went on Robbie, "I leave to-morrow for Virginia. Will you meet me at the bank at 10:30, and identify me so that I can get that check cashed?"

"Sure," replied his friend.

"Sure?"

"Bet on it!" answered Cullen, slapping him on the shoulder.

"Gentlemen, good-night!" said Robbie, and with this remark he turned and walked away.

At 10:30 the next day he cashed his check. At eleven o'clock he was on the train, seated with his mother and sister

It was his intention ere he left to have called at his office and inform his clerk that he was going away. He arose late and did not take the time. His friend Cullen volunteered to go there during the day and say that Mr. Porter wanted his mail sent to Fredericksburg, Virginia.

Without accident or delay the little party arrived about six o'clock in that very hotel in which more than twenty years ago Robbie Porter and Judge Bowers had dined together.

The past came before him as he stepped to the desk and registered:

"Robert Porter,

"Lydia Porter,

"Sarah Porter,

"New York."

Robbie's dress and liberal use of "tips" procured him the attention of the entire house.

The best rooms were at his disposal, and a colored servant was always at his elbow.

The day had passed pleasantly, and the cheerfulness of his conversation had a wonderful effect upon the two women. They had become bright, smiling. Mrs. Porter's gloom had almost gone. The wonderful restoration of a son, long since almost forgotten, filled her withered heart with joy. His encouraging assurance that her crime was beyond the pale of the law seemed to have taken from her a great weight. Her features had relaxed, her form was more erect, and her conversation had lost its melancholy tone. It was a joy to feel that at last, though in the close of life, a champion had come to console her past, to cheer her present, and provide for her future. It was a sweet, delicious feeling, the first she had known for years, when she contemplated this sturdy, calm but earnest advocate. That he was her son, too, intensified this feeling. To her he was already, though known but a few hours, the noblest man she had ever met. She was proud of his every act and word. His tenderness, his solicitation, the royal entertainment he afforded on the journey, bespoke him what he was, a liberal, big-hearted gentleman.

With a thousand dollars in his pocket, Robbie exhibited the prodigality of a king.

The morning sun had not reached the meridian when an open carriage, the best in all Fredericksburg that could be hired, drawn by a pair of horses, occupied by Robbie Porter, his mother and sister, stopped just before it reached the old gate that opened out upon the road leading down to the river at River View.

When the vehicle stopped the stillness was almost supreme.

It was the second day of May.

Every dogwood tree was white with blossoms, and the soft zephyr that gently stirred them spread their delicate odors about the scene. Way up, toward the sky, the green-topped pines swayed in splendid majesty. The warm sunbeams penetrated the rifts of verdant foliage, and ever and anon the muffled sound of rippling water could be heard.

"Wait!" said Robbie, addressing the driver, and preparing to dismount. "Wait here! Put up the top, and shade the ladies. I will go forward and see who now lives here. This is the place, mother!"

On the way they had met few travelers, and made no inquiries. The driver, a young colored man, of whom Robbie asked some questions, admitted that he was a stranger "in deseparts," and did not know who lived there.

"I'll find out and come back soon," he exclaimed, and proceeded along the road to the big gate.

After his experience of the preceding night, Robbie was prepared, he imagined, for all kinds of situations. Controlling his emotions, and resolving to maintain a quiet, calm demeanor, no matter what revelations he learned, he approached the familiar entrance to the lawn.

Once or twice he stopped and surveyed the charming scene. To his eye there was no change since he had ridden away that wet morning in November. Then he feasted on hopes. Now he was returning to feed on memories.

How familiar and how inviting everything about him! There was the same old oak, extending its long and tortuous branches across the road, over the fence, so that it shaded the green lawn. Why, there, a little distance through the woods, was that same pond, whose beautiful lilies he had so often gathered for Phœbe. Through spaces between the trees as he passed along he caught glimpses of the rolling river. There was that same little island, looking like a green mound, where he and Phœbe had so often wandered.

All the past was coming back.

All the sweetnesses of his life in this hallowed spot. All of the happy days, all of the delicious nights, when he sat on the river bank and repeated to Phœbe the story of Dido, who stood upon the sad seashore "and waved her love to come again to Carthage." He remembered the goodness of Uncle Phineas, the gentleness, the patient kindness of Aunt Rachel. He knew now, what he didn't know then, how blessed he was. He had gone forth to battle with the world. True, he achieved his purposes, yet he felt the world had been the conqueror.

Was Phœbe alive? Did she live here now under another name? Would she know him? What would she say to him? Would she charge him with inconstancy? No! surely not that. Had he not written and rewritten to her? Had she not scorned his love by a silence more cruel, more crushing than open denunciation? He loved her then. He had always loved her. "And by heavens!" he spoke aloud, "I love her still!"

He stopped. His hand was on the old gate. He looked along the graveled drive and saw the white walls, the tall, square pillars and the red chimneys of the old house. How beautiful that terraced lawn, how tasteful the shrubbery, how neat the trees! Why, the old gate had been just "whitewashed." To Robbie's wondering eyes everything looked very much as it did the first day he marched, sore and dust covered, under those shady trees.

The appearance of the place filled him with more concern than he cared to confess. The hand of Phineas Strong was seen in all its appointments.

No stranger could have in tree, in house, in lawn, in neatness and taste, so completely reflected the character and work of his former benefactor. His hand was on the gate latch, but he hesitated.

"Nonsense!" he finally muttered to himself. "The old man must have been dead these ten years. Why, he would be past ninety now. Oh, no, Phœbe may live here, but her father is dead."

He opened the gate and entered. He now walked more rapidly toward the house, stopping but once to pluck a sweet-smelling shrub from an overhanging bush. The nearer he drew to that wide and inviting porch, with its tall square pillars, the more evident became his agitation, and in spite of himself his heart began a throbbing that threatened displacement. The familiar distinctness of everything startled, unnerved him. The old walnut tree, the boxwood bush at the stone step of the veranda, the iron mud scraper, made of an old horseshoe; the honeysuckle vine, in full bloom, and winding itself in rich luxuriance around the pillars and among the lattice work; all there, just as they were twenty-eight years ago.

He stepped upon the hard oak flooring, spotless in its smooth whiteness, and made two or three strides for the old doorway. The stillness was broken by a gentle rustling among the stray branches of the honeysuckle vine, and Robbie turned to look whence it came.

SHE SPOKE, AND THE VOICE WAS THE VOICE OF PHŒBE STRONG.

He was, he thought, prepared for surprises, but what he now saw took from him the power of thought or action.   There, not twenty feet away, stood with her back toward him, evidently unaware of his presence, the form of a young woman.   Her size, her shape, her pose, the luxuriant braids that hung down her back, her little feet, the hand with which she turned a supple branch between the lattices, her drab dress, everything, the counterpart of his beloved Phœbe.   For a full minute he stood transfixed.   His breath came hard and fast, and finally, with a mighty effort, came back the power to move, to speak.   With a bound he was at her side.   His silk hat fell upon the oaken floor.   His arms parted, and in an instant the lovely form was folded in them, tight to his throbbing bosom.   One word, almost shouted, escaped his lips, "Phœbe!"

A scream, a wild cry of fright, resounded through the air. Quick as a flash the young girl had broken from that strong embrace, and darting to the furtherest corner of the porch, her eyes flashing, her bosom heaving, and her face vermilion, she stood in an attitude of defiance, her expression mixed with wonder, indignation and pain.   It was lucky, perhaps, she had the power of speech, or heaven knows how long Robbie Porter would have stood there, mute, bewildered.   He saw his mistake; the creature was not Phœbe.   She had blue eyes, and now, he could see, her hair was not black, but dark brown.   She spoke, and the voice was the voice of Phœbe Strong.

"Thou art evidently laboring under some mistake!"

she said, her face softening a little, and her attitude assuming a less defiant position as she saw the stranger made no motion to advance.

Poor Robbie! for once in his life it looked as though all his resources were about to fail. He rallied, however, forced a smile, bowed and said:

"I ask your pardon. I am mistaken."

He picked up his hat and continued, sadly, kindly, "Do I look like a crazy man?"

His face betrayed his sincerity, and his voice appealed to her, touched her. There was so much of pathos in it. It reassured her, won her sympathy.

"No;" she spoke frankly, clearly. "Thee looks like a gentleman in the full possession of his senses."

"Thanks. I took you for an old friend of mine. Of course, now I see my mistake. But your profile as you appeared to me, was exactly as she looked the first day I saw her, right about where you were standing. Her name was Phœbe Strong. Perhaps you are her daughter?"

"I am her daughter," said the young girl. She was sad now.

"Yes, I could swear to that. But her eyes are brown. Yours are patches of Italian skies. Will you permit me to present you my card?"

He handed her one from his case. She glanced at it, dropped it on the floor, and darted away like a frightened deer. He heard her feet in the old hall; he heard a door open, and heard her call:

"Grandfather! Grandfather! Grandmother! Grandmother! come quick, oh, come, come quick! everybody come! Robert Porter is on the front porch!"

He heard a moving of chairs, a shuffling of feet, and presently in the wide, old doorway, his form bent, his snow-white hair falling in thin locks over his shoulders, his hands trembling, clasped one over the other over the end of a cane, on which he leaned for support, he beheld his old friend, Phineas Strong. The slumbering affection of nearly thirty years awoke in his heart, and became again a living love. He caught the tottering, trembling form in his arms:

"Oh, Uncle Phineas, doesn't thee know me? Doesn't thee know Robbie Porter? Look up! I am Robbie!"

The old man straightened his bent form, drew partly away, shaded his eyes with his hands, gazed a moment, dropped his cane; his voice was almost choked with emotion as he spoke:

"The grave does give up the dead. Yes, it is thee. It is Robert Porter. A chair, Phœbe!"

Gently Robbie eased him into it, stooped, and placed his cane in his wrinkled, withered hand.

"Thee hardly knows me, Robert!" the old man went on. "My days are nearly done. Thee is not dead. Did thee know I tried to save thy life twenty years ago on the Lancaster race track?"

"Yes," said Robbie.

"Thee didn't die of the accident?"

"No. I recovered."

"Why didn't thee come home? Didn't the woman who waited on thee tell thee—tell thee about Phœbe?"

"Thee means Josephine Bowers?"

"That was the name—did she tell thee?"

"She told me," said Robbie, "that thee said thee never wanted to see my face again. That thee had come there for revenge, but that the Lord had relieved thee of thy chance.

"I longed to come back. Had I not met with the accident I should have started that very night. I had written, and rewritten to Phœbe, yet she never replied. I was, however, bound to have an explanation, but when I heard what thee had said I thought it useless. I left Lancaster as soon as I was able. I have never been to the place since."

"Thee tells strange things, Robert. We got a letter from the woman; it's about the house now, saying thee had died in a hospital. She sent thy clothes, some books, thy silver watch, and some other things. They are in thy old room yet, I reckon."

"Did she do that?" Robbie's voice was cold, bitter now. A light was coming to him.

Josephine Bowers loved him.

In twenty years his knowledge of women had become greatly extended. He began to understand some things.

"Tell me, Uncle Phineas, did— did Phœbe write to me?"

"More than twenty times, Robbie. She loved thee devotedly. She could not understand it."

"Oh, Uncle Phineas!" cried Robbie. "I see it all now. She did it—she stole the letters. She got

she loved thee as her own.   For twenty years she has
been thy defender.   Bring her, Phœbe.   I want to see
her smile again before I die."

Phœbe, whose eyes were riveted upon her father's
handsome form and kind face, flew away in search of
Rachel Strong.

CHAPTER LI.

MEANWHILE the ladies waited in the carriage. The sun's heat became uncomfortably oppressive. Thirst, curiosity, finally nervousness, at last prompted them to order the driver to proceed. The poor old mother was seized with fearful apprehensions. Trouble in her life had so often been her portion, she looked for it here. The shroud of sorrow had enveloped her whole life. It was not likely it would be lifted now.

The carriage halted under the walnut tree, not more than forty feet from the scene just described. Both ladies alighted.

It chanced at that very moment, Rachel Strong, now long past her eightieth year, a large straw sun hat half concealing her face, was plucking some blossoms from a lilac tree. The spectacle of a carriage, from which two strange ladies were just alighting, was sufficient to not only arrest her attention, but fill her with the liveliest emotions of wonder and concern. It was a rare thing to see visitors at River View nowadays. Her placid face, sweetened and softened by the hand of time, was full of gentle wonder as her feeble steps took the direction leading to the carriage.

Having never seen Sarah, she, of course, did not know her. The memory of Lydia Langdon was long

ago departed, and in the wrinkled face, stooping form
and snow-white hair of the elder woman there was not
a feature not a vestige to remind her of her once young
and beautiful rival.

She, therefore, approached and addressed them pleasantly.

At the sound of that voice Lydia Porter was seized
with a sudden weakness in all her limbs. She turned
and clutched at Sarah to support her wavering form.
One look was sufficient. Time had dealt gently with
Rachel. Her eyes had not lost their freshness; mental
torment had not soured her face. It was the face of
long ago, in a subdued coloring, in another frame.

Face to face, at last, after fifty years of sorrowing
wonder, after half a century of deep remorse, horrible,
haunting dreams, misgivings, regrets, two women,
each responsible for all the grief and woe the other had
known, gazed one upon the other.

In a minute, less than a minute, Lydia was kneeling
in the dust, clasping the knees of Rachel Strong.

"Oh, Rachel! Rachel! Have mercy! don't tell!
forgive me! forgive me! I wronged thee, but my
punishment has been great; my penitence sincere."

Poor, poor, frightened sinner. The terror in her
upturned face, the pleading, hopeless look would have
touched a harder heart than ever beat in Rachel Strong's
bosom. Years ago she had made her peace, had for-
given Lydia, had tried to think that after all she had
been harsh to the poor girl; often regretted, not only
her awful scheme of vengeance, but bitterly reproached

herself for allowing a helpless girl to go forth from her house alone.

She did not, at first, comprehend the sudden scene she was witnessing. She had tried so to forget that little past in her life. By degrees, however, her mental faculties were aroused. She was conscious now. The kneeling, haggard, haunted woman at her feet was Lydia Langdon. Her poor old hands reached down and rested upon the shoulders of her former rival.

"Rise, Lydia. It is thee. I see thee plain now. Rise and let me kneel to thee and beg forgiveness. Forgive me, Lydia. My cruel revenge has cost me many a sigh, and in thy face I see fifty years of suffering. I deceived thee with the most heartless lie that was ever uttered. I tortured thee into flight. I have prayed that I might meet thee and tell thee, before thee dies, thou art no murderess. I heard the child cry, and saved its life. Phineas buried an empty trunk."

From the lips of Lydia Porter there escaped one long cry, a cry of joy:

"Oh, God! God!" she exclaimed, looking with uplifted hands, "I thank thee! I thank thee! My daughter, my daughter, my first-born. Tell me where she is, lead me to her, and I'll forgive thee, worship thee! Tell me, Rachel, did she really live?"

"She lived. I raised her as my own. But I hated thee that night. I feared to tell thee the truth, lest thee would not go. I did not tell Phineas for days. I had my revenge! but the Lord softened my anger, and Phineas won back my love."

"But the child, where is she; does she know, does she know that thee is not her real mother?"

"She knew nothing. She knows nothing. She is dead, Lydia. Here comes Phœbe, her daughter."

Phœbe now came hurriedly toward them, panting with excitement, and exclaiming:

"Come, grandmother, come, quick! My father is alive; he is here; he is on the porch talking to grandfather. Oh, come!"

"Phœbe! Phœbe!" said Aunt Rachel, "is thee crazy? Doesn't thee see we have company? Thy father, child. Don't talk so!"

"But it is so. Grandfather said so; said the grave had given up the dead!"

She had seized her grandmother's hands in her exciting impulsiveness, and strove to drag her toward the house.

"Come, do come! All of you come."

Thus urged and entreated, Phœbe leading the way, the four ladies soon came upon the porch, face to face with Phineas Strong and Robbie Porter.

The scene that immediately ensued almost beggars description.

"Aunt Rachel," exclaimed Robbie, springing forward and gathering her dear old form in his arms.

"Lydia!" gasped Phineas Strong, rising, trembling like a leaf, his eyes staring wildly, his hand shading them, and the color faded from his face.

"Lydia," he repeated slowly, lowering his hand. "Lydia Langdon. I believe in the resurrection!"

But Lydia Langdon heard him not.   The sudden
meaning of young Phœbe's declaration, "My father is
here," came to her.   Film filled her eyes.   Darkness
fell around her; her limbs grew rigid, paralyzed.   Her
brain swam, her body surged to and fro, and then,
before any one could stay her form, she lunged forward, and fell upon her face upon the hard oaken
boards in a dead faint.

Introductions were overlooked, formality ceased.
Salutations were suspended and the whole house was
employed in efforts to restore the poor woman to consciousness.

Tenderly Robbie took her in his arms, gently he laid
her upon that old sofa in the front room—the very one
he had once slept upon nearly thirty years ago.   Gradually she revived, wearily opened her eyes.   Around
her stood Phineas Strong, Aunt Rachel, and Robbie.
She looked first at one, and then at the other.   Eagerly
she scanned each face.   Rachel's was the only one that
answered her searching gaze.   At last she spoke:

"Phineas, does thee know—know," pointing toward
Robbie with her bony fingers, "this is my son?"

"There! there," said Phineas, whose greatest surprise was yet to come.   "Thee wanders."

"No! no!" she replied.   "Would to heaven I did.
Tell him, Robert."

The horrible revelation which had come to Lydia,
the shock of which had deprived her of reason, was
still concealed from Robbie and Phineas.   Robbie's
answer, therefore, produced upon his old friend an

effect very near that from which his mother was just recovering. Confident that there were no other startling surprises to follow, he proceeded to say:

"Yes, Uncle Phineas, she is my mother!"

The old man straightened his tall form, and his face assumed a horrible, ghastly look. His lower jaw dropped, and for a moment it looked as though he would sink to the floor.

"Thy mother!—Great God, have I lived to see this day, to hear this thing. Robert, is this true?"

"True, Uncle Phineas."

"Then," he spoke, slowly, sadly, "Robert, thou art looking upon the most miserable sinner that ever disgraced the earth. Ninety years have I lived, but this day have I drank of the cup of bitterness. Robbie, if this is true, thou art thy Phœbe's half-brother, for this woman of a truth is her mother!"

"Uncle Phineas! Uncle Phineas! Aunt Rachel!" cried Robbie, looking first at one and then the other. "It cannot be. This is a horrible dream."

"Oh, Robbie!" said Rachel, going up to him, "would that it was. It is, alas, too true!"

"And Phœbe's father is——"

"Thy Uncle Phineas!" she replied.

"Good God!" exclaimed Robbie. "Can human endurance survive this dreadful truth?"

"And I," almost moaned Phineas Strong, "I am the guilty wretch who has done this thing. Smite me, Robert! Smite me! Heaven will forgive the deed. I have lived too long. Lived to confess that I am a scoundrel; lived to know that the little goodness I have done cannot outweigh the awful misery I have caused; cannot wipe out the stain, the disgrace, the horrible effects of my great sin.

"Oh, Robert, my sin I thought twofold; but, alas, it is fourfold. I ruined a young and innocent girl; I deceived and dishonored the noblest, sweetest wife man ever had; I drove my ruined victim into the street; and now, now through me, my sin, is disclosed the awful truth that forever disgraces thee and thy child. Let me die!"

He turned to his weeping wife, bowed his head upon her shoulder and wept like a child. "Thee was right, Rachel, chickens come home to roost."

"Chickens come home to roost," repeated Aunt Rachel.

"Chickens come home to roost," sighed poor Lydia Langdon.

"Chickens come home to roost," said Robbie Porter, leaning against the wall, and with mist-dimmed eyes sadly surveying the scene.

．　　．　　．　　．　　．　　．　　．

There is little more to be told. By degrees the effect of the matters just related wore away, and tranquillity returned. What you and I know, reader, was soon, in every detail, disclosed. From the new Phœbe it was agreed some of the matters had best be concealed. Phineas Strong was soon made acquainted with all the circumstances that induced Robbie to return to Virginia.

From an old bookcase he produced the lying letter of Josephine Bowers.

From the old attic, in his father's old knapsack, Robbie brought its contents, and among them, yellow with age, was found his mother's marriage certificate. It had lain there, undiscovered, for nearly thirty years.

In the afternoon, Phineas, with Rachel on his arm, Robbie, with his mother, Sarah and the new Phœbe, already proud of her handsome father, visited the little burying ground. At the grave of the color bearer Lydia Langdon knelt. Before his beloved Phœbe's, Robbie stood with uncovered head, while a flood of recollections rolled before his vision.

"Here," said Phineas Strong, "at the graves of the brave, the beloved dead, let us bury all the past. Let us forgive one another, as we hope forgiveness hereafter. To the most of us, our remaining days are few. While they last let us try to be happy. Robert, Lydia, Sarah, I have enough for all. Let this hereafter be your abiding-place. To-morrow, Robbie, thee can draw a deed, quit claim, for thy mother to execute. My will gives the place to Phœbe, so I want her to have an unclouded title. Though I guess the statutes of limitation would defeat thy dower suit; however, the law can do no more than we ourselves can do. Prepare the deed, and I will immediately settle fifteen thousand dollars upon thy mother. Is that fair?'

"More than fair, Uncle Phineas," replied Robbie. "Thee was always good. We may yet see happy days."

As to Robbie, the invitation to remain at River View

met with his entire approval. He decided at once to accept. Sarah, however, returned to her advertising business in New York, there to sound the praises of her brother Robert, leaving her mother happier than she had ever known her.

A few weeks after his return, Robbie and his daughter Phœbe made a visit to Fredericksburg. At the post office he was presented with letters forwarded to him from New York. One of them was a large, bulky package. He opened it, and once more his nerves sustained a shock. It was the following:

"LANCASTER, Pa., April 30, 1890.
"ROBERT PORTER, Esq., New York City.
"SIR: We beg leave to inform you that after much effort and expense, we have come to the conclusion that you are the Robert Porter for whom we advertised about a year ago. Investigation which we have made confirms us to the extent that we feel safe in saying that if you can come here with proofs as to your identity, you will be declared the sole legatee by will of the late Josephine Bowers, a widow lady who died a year ago, leaving an estate valued at two hundred thousand dollars. It was her dying request that the enclosed packet of letters should be sent you the minute you were found. If you can come here at once, do so."
"Yours truly,   RICH & STONE."

One glance at the dozen faded letters was enough.

They were his letters to Phœbe, and one or two from Phœbe to him. They seemed like messages from the dead.

In a few weeks there appeared over the grave of the color bearer an appropriate tombstone. Upon it was inscribed:

"Sacred to the memory
of
BENJAMIN PORTER,
Who lost his life displaying his
Country's flag upon the field of battle."

His widow and his son have erected this stone to commemorate his valor, and as a testimonial of their affection.

Over the grave of the once beauteous Phœbe now stands a marble shaft, whose polished sides are still shining in the sun.

"Wife," "Daughter," "Mother," in letters large and clear are carved upon it.

On one side this inscription appears:

"Sacred to the memory
of
PHŒBE STRONG PORTER.

———

"Her life was like a flower, pure, sweet and fragrant. Like a flower she faded. It is the belief of those whose love hath caused this stone to be erected, that like a flower she blooms again, now, in the gardens of eternity, where the seeds of affection never die, and the roses of hope never perish."

———

CONCLUSION.

Among the faded and yellow letters Robbie received was one which for several days failed for some reason to be noticed. It looked more fresh than the others, and the superscription was in a different handwriting from Phœbe's. How it escaped his attention he could not understand. It was sealed and marked "To be opened only by Robbie Porter." He tore away the envelope, and this is what he found within:

"DEAR ROBERT: Physicians tell me that I must soon die. I cannot, therefore, meet you here face to face. It was for years my hope, my dream, that fate or chance would throw us again together. That dream is now dispelled; that hope is dead. For nineteen years I have lived a life of misery. I have endured all the pangs remorse can bring; have suffered the never-dying humiliation of a despised love. For I loved you.

"Jealousy prompted me to conspire against the sweet object of your affection. My love for you made me mad. I burned some of her letters and retained yours. In the hope that you would love me, I invented a base lie about your dear uncle. Your rage, your resentment will be kindled against me. Forgiveness you can never grant. My own passion has shown me how deeply I injured you, how cruelly I wronged her, and how utterly despicable was my crime. In the hope of softening your anger, I have made you my heir. Everything is yours, even the judge's library you so highly prized. I have learned that wealth and position, without love and goodness, are useless acquisitions. I hope you will spend my money in princely prodigality; and in the luxuries it may supply, forget the sin of poor Josephine Bowers, whose one base act has blasted forever all her hopes of happiness beyond the grave.

"Sure enough, as you said your Aunt Rachel used to say:

"'Chickens Come Home to Roost.'"

THE END.

www.ingramcontent.com/pod-product-compliance
Lightning Source LLC
Chambersburg PA
CBHW021126270326
41929CB00009B/1067